Prima Games
An Imprint of Random H...

BATTLEFIELD BAD COMPANY

PRIMA OFFICIAL GAME GUIDE

WRITTEN BY
MICHAEL KNIGHT

Senior Product Manager: Mario De Govia
Associate Product Manager: Rebecca Chastain
Copyeditor: Julia Kilmer
Design and Layout: Calibre Grafix, LLC
Manufacturing: Suzanne Goodwin

Important:

Prima Games would like to thank Brad Bennett and Gustav Enekull for all their assistance.

Author Acknowledgments:
I would like to thank both Rebecca Chastain and Mario de Govia at Prima Games for all their help in making this book a reality. I also want to express my love and appreciate to my wife Trisa and our children—Beth, Sarah, Connor, Tanner, Paige, and Nathan—for their understanding as Dad was looking all over for gold bars.

ABOUT THE AUTHOR

Michael Knight has worked in the computer/video game industry since 1994 and has been an author with Prima Games for ten years, writing over 60 guides during this time. Michael has used both his degree in Military History and experience as a high school teacher to formulate and devise effective strategies and tactics for hit titles such as the Tom Clancy's Rainbow Six and Hitman series. He has also authored several titles in the *Star Wars* universe including *Star Wars Republic Commando*, *Star Wars Episode III: Revenge of the Sith*, *Star Wars Battlefront II*, and *Star Wars: Empire at War*. Michael has also developed scenarios/missions and written game manuals for SSI, Red Storm Entertainment, and Novalogic.

When he is not busy at work on an upcoming strategy guide, Michael likes to spend time with his wife and six children at their home in Northern California. It was with their help that Michael used his abilities and experience to write three travel/strategy guides on Disneyland and Southern California, in which he developed tips and hints to help vacationing families save time and money while maximizing their fun.

We want to hear from you! E-mail comments and feedback to mknight@primagames.com.

ISBN: 978-0-7615-5909-2
Library of Congress Catalog Card Number: 2008920422
Printed in the United States of America

08 09 10 11 LL 10 9 8 7 6 5 4 3 2 1

★ CONTENTS ★

WELCOME TO B-COMPANY

Welcome to the 222nd Army battalion, B-Company. This is where the Army rakes together all the insubordinates, hell raisers, and troublemakers that won't fit in any other unit. When the Rangers and Deltas are too expensive to waste, these guys are the first ones in.

They're called "Bad Company": a mismatched bunch of rejects selected to serve their country as cannon fodder. This isn't the kind of outfit a lot of soldiers would join voluntarily. Getting transferred to "the B" is a punishment and a way for the generals to put all their rotten eggs in one basket.

No one starts out in Bad Company. But for some, this is where they end up....

NOTE ★★

During the single-player campaign, you are a member of Bad Company. You play as one of the squad with three AI-controlled squad mates. While you have no direct control over the members of your squad and can't give them orders or commands, they usually follow you around and add their fire support as needed to help you accomplish your objectives.

PRESTON MARLOWE

I'm Preston Marlowe.

You know, when I was growing up all I ever wanted to be was a soldier. Runs in the family, I guess. My dad was in Vietnam. My grandfather fought the Nazis. Me, I couldn't wait to get out there and fight for truth, justice, and the American way.

The reality of life in the Army didn't really hit me until they shipped us to Europe. And as it turned out, war can be pretty boring. At least when you're stuck at a base in the middle of nowhere waiting for orders. I had

to do something to distract myself, right? And if I had landed that chopper just a few yards to the left nobody would have noticed....

NOTE ★★

Preston Marlowe is the player's character during the single-player campaign. You usually begin each mission with an M416 assault rifle with attached grenade launcher as well as an auto-injector for healing yourself. However, you are able to pick up weapons and gadgets you find during the mission as well as weapons dropped by dead enemies. So even though Marlowe is an assault class soldier by default, you can use the weapons and equipment of the various other classes.

★ SARGE ★

Sergeant Samuel D. Redford reporting for duty.

They tell me I'm the first soldier ever to be transferred to Bad Company on my own request. Doesn't surprise me. This outfit has the highest mortality rate in the Army. We're just target practice for the enemy, really.

Believe me, I know I'm playing against the odds. But if the deal I made can get me out of this damned war, then it's worth the risk.

You know, I used to love the Army. I was proud to serve my country. Not any more. A couple of weeks more, and I'm out of here. The only things I'm planning to fight then are marlin and bluefin tuna.

NOTE ★★

Sarge is the leader of Bad Company. While he is a straight shooter, a by-the-book type of non-commissioned officer, Sarge is loyal to his men and will not hesitate to step across a line (or international border) to protect one of his squad. Sarge is the typical assault class soldier and carries an assault rifle with an attached grenade launcher.

prprimagames.com

HAGGARD

Hey, Haggard here.

Don't let the rugged handsome looks fool ya. I'm just your average, normal G.I., really. I'm a great people person. And when they say that folk tend to get killed around me, that's just not true. Well, I mean...we're at war, you know.

So shit happens, I guess. What else? I enjoy fine food, especially beer and beef jerky. Also, I like blowing stuff up. Back home everyone was kinda giving me a hard time about that, but in the Army they actually want you to blow stuff up, so I fit right in.

OK, looking back, that thing with the Officers' latrine and the Claymores was a mistake, maybe. But, still, it blew up real nice!

NOTE ★★

Haggard is the squad demolitions soldier. He carries a shotgun as well as an anti-tank rocket launcher. When facing an enemy vehicle, Haggard is the one you want next to you. Maybe it is all the loud explosions he has been exposed to, but there is something about Haggard that makes the squad wonder if he is all there. In fact, they even entertain thoughts that he is just plain...well, let's just say "eccentric."

SWEETWATER

My name is Private Terrence Sweetwater.

I don't mind telling you that all this soldiering crap really freaks me out. I'm not cut out for this. An Army tour seemed like an easy way to get the scholarship I needed. But with my skills and knowledge, I figured I wouldn't have to do any actual fighting.

Turns out I figured wrong. 'Cause here I am—in Bad Company. And, boy, did they get that name right! In fact, the company is so bad that sometimes I think I'm more likely to get killed by my own squad than by the enemy. That kinda sucks. But, still, we do get some good toys. Did you see that new laser designator? Pretty cool, eh?

NOTE ★★

Sweetwater is the squad support soldier. He carries a light machine gun that can put out a lot of firepower and is great when engaging enemy infantry. Sweetwater is also technologically savvy. Listen to his comments during a mission. He often has good suggestions about how to accomplish an objective—you just have to pay attention and listen for his bits of wisdom hidden among the whining.

PRIMA Official Game Guide

BAD COMPANY
BATTLEFIELD

BASIC TRAINING

Training prepares you for combat situations like this.

Okay, soldier. Now that you have met the squad, let's go over some of the basics. Even though you have been through the Army's basic training program, the fact that you are in Bad Company means that some of the things you were taught didn't stick. We are not concerned about military discipline and decorum. Bad Company doesn't care if you shine your boots or press your BDUs. The basics we want to review are all related to combat since you see an awful lot of it in this squad.

★ THE HEADS UP DISPLAY ★

The heads up display, or HUD, is the way that vital information is displayed on your screen. None of the items on your HUD are there for aesthetics. They are there to help you accomplish your mission and keep you alive.

RETICLE

The reticle is always located in the center of the screen. It usually consists of a circle with a small pip in the middle. The reticle is the aiming point for your weapon. To hit a target, place the pip over it. Notice that the color of the pip changes depending on the target. It will turn orange when placed over an enemy and blue when centered on a friendly unit.

NOTE ★ ★

Some weapons, such as sniper rifles, do not have a reticle. Instead, they must be aimed using ironsights. Other weapons, such as grenade launchers or other weapons that lob a projectile feature a reticle with a vertical line of arrows for aiming at various ranges.

★ TIP ★

When firing at an enemy, watch for an orange semicircle to appear under your pip. This means you are hitting the target, though not necessarily indicating a kill. This is especially useful when making long-range shots.

MINIMAP

Located in the bottom-left corner of the screen, the minimap provides a top-down, 360-degree view of the environment through which you are moving. The minimap rotates as you change direction so that the top of the minimap is always the direction you are currently facing. The letter "N" designates the direction of north to help you maintain your bearing. In addition to showing the terrain, the minimap also shows the location of all detected enemies as orange dots or orange vehicle icons. Friendly units are displayed in blue, and empty vehicles are represented by white icons. It is a good idea to constantly refer to the minimap to keep track of enemies. Even if you can't see them visually, the minimap lets

you know where they are located, whether behind a hill or inside a building. The minimap also comes in handy when looking for ammo. The icon with three bullets represents an ammo box while white an X shows you where you can pick up weapons or gadgets. Finally, orange triangles show you the location of objectives.

★ TIP ★

The color of the ground on the minimap also has meaning. The red shaded terrain is out of bounds. If you move into the red area, you have five seconds to get back into the gray or you will be killed by enemy artillery. Just remember to "Stay in the Gray."

HEALTH AND AMMO COUNTERS

Located in the bottom-right corner of the screen are a couple of counters. The top counter, next to a medical cross icon, lists your health as a percentage. Full health is 100 percent. As you take damage, your health percentage counts down. When it reaches 0, you are dead. Immediately below the health counter and next to a bullet icon is your ammo counter. Your ammo is represented by two numbers. The number to the left of the vertical line is the number of rounds you currently have loaded in the weapon, while the number to the right is the amount of ammo not currently in your weapon and available for reload. As you reload your weapon, the number on the right decreases as the number on the left increases up to the maximum amount the weapon can hold.

★ TIP ★

Keep an eye on both ammo numbers. Make sure the left number is close to maximum before you get into a fight. If the number on the right gets low, start looking for an ammo box for a resupply.

CONTEXTUAL ACTIONS

During gameplay, you have the opportunity to interact with some objects. At these times, instructions appear on the screen. For example, when you are near a weapon on the ground or next to a vehicle not occupied by enemies, a note appears at the bottom center of the screen stating which button you need to press to pick up the weapon or to get into the vehicle. Other instructions appear along the right side of the screen when operating a vehicle or using a new weapon, informing you how to accomplish different actions.

primagames.com

SOLDIER CONTROLS

MOVEMENT

You have to move to get where you need to go.

Moving around the battlefield is fairly straightforward. The left stick controls forward and backward movement as well as strafing to the left and right. Strafing is a sideways move where the direction you are facing does not change. It is useful for moving out from cover to fire, then back behind cover for protection. The right stick controls where you look—turning left and right as well as looking up and down.

CROUCHING AND SPRINTING

Crouch down so you can take advantage of low cover, like these stone walls.

There is more to movement than just walking. Press the left stick to crouch down. While crouched, you move slower. However, since you are lower, you make a smaller target for the enemy to hit and you can more easily duck behind cover. When advancing against an enemy position, it is usually best to move crouched, as it is harder for the enemy to detect you.

At times, it is better to move fast. Hold down the left stick while moving to sprint. You can't use weapons or equipment while sprinting, but you are much more difficult for the enemy to hit. Use sprinting when you have to cross a dangerously open piece of ground as you move from one position of cover to another.

COMBAT

This entire game is about combat.

While moving about the battlefield is a major part of gameplay, the sole purpose of movement is to place you in a position where you can use your weapons to engage and eliminate the enemy. As a member of Bad Company, you have access to different types of weapons. However, the controls for using these weapons are fairly common. For specifics on weapons, see the Infantry chapter, which covers this topic in greater detail.

As mentioned earlier, the reticle in the center of the screen is your aiming point for using weapons. Most of the weapons you use are direct fire, meaning that the projectile you fire travels in a basically straight line from your weapon to the target. Using these weapons is simple. Place the pip of the reticule directly over the target, then press the fire button. For semi-automatic or single-shot weapons such as pistols, shotguns, and sniper rifles, each time you press the fire button, you fire a single round. However, for automatic weapons such as submachine guns, assault rifles, and light machine guns, they will continue to shoot as you hold down the fire button until they are empty.

When firing automatic weapons, the longer the burst, the less accurate the fire. Therefore, to maintain greater accuracy and still put out a lot of lead, fire in short bursts. You are more likely to kill your target, especially at medium to long range, with a few accurate rounds rather than an entire clip spread all over.

USING WEAPONS

You have weapons that cause a lot of damage.

IRONSIGHTS AND SCOPES

Ironsights is best for medium- to long-range fire.

PRIMA Official Game Guide

BATTLEFIELD BAD COMPANY

When you fire a weapon using the reticle to aim, you are essentially firing from the hip, with the butt of your weapon in the crook of your arm. This is not very accurate and should only be used at close range. To increase your accuracy, press the zoom button. This will bring up the ironsights view, where you are actually looking through the weapon's sight to aim. The butt of the weapon is brought up to your shoulder giving you greater accuracy. If your weapon is equipped with a scope, the zoom button will provide a view through the scope rather than ironsights.

TIP

It is a good idea to get in the habit of pressing the zoom button to bring up your ironsights before firing. This not only is more accurate, but it also provides a zoomed-in view of the target. To further increase accuracy, crouch down and remain stationary while firing.

GRENADES AND GRENADE LAUNCHERS

Throw hand grenades farther by holding down the fire button and aiming up.

Most primary weapons come in a package with grenades or, in the case of the assault rifle, a grenade launcher. If carrying a sniper rifle, you get a pistol instead. Grenades require a bit more skill to use effectively since they are either thrown or launched. Unlike a bullet or rocket which travels in a straight line for the purpose of gameplay, grenades travel in a parabolic arc due to their lower speed and the effect of gravity. In the case of a grenade launcher, the farther away you are from the target, the higher you need to aim. That is why the reticle for a grenade launcher has several aiming points along a vertical line. For a short-range shot, use the top aiming point. The farther away your target, the lower the aiming point you should use. By using a lower aiming point, you are essentially aiming the weapon up higher to lob the grenade toward the target.

Hand grenades work a bit differently. They are thrown rather than launched and you don't get a reticle for aiming. Instead, the longer you hold down the fire button, the farther you throw. A quick press of the fire button will toss the grenade right in front of you while a long hold on the fire button before release will send it flying some distance. The farther your target, the higher you should aim your throw.

NOTE ★ ★

When using grenades, it is important to understand how they work. Rifle grenades fired from a launcher explode on impact. Hand grenades, in contrast, have a five second fuse. As a result, you can throw hand grenades around a corner.

★ VEHICLES ★

Tanks are the king of vehicles.

The maps are often quite large. It can take a while to walk them on foot. Therefore, use vehicles to get around. There are several types of vehicles in the game, yet they all are driven with similar controls. The left stick controls motion while the right stick controls the view. However, in the case of infantry fighting vehicles (IFVs) and tanks, the right stick controls the turret rather than steering the vehicle.

Boats are a good way to get around a map where there are waterways.

All vehicles have more than one seat. When you get into an empty vehicle, you are placed in the driver's seat by default. However, you can press the change seat button to move to another position inside the vehicle. The driver has control of a vehicle's movement and, in the tanks and IFVs, also controls the vehicle's main weapon. The second position is usually a machine gun. Some vehicles even have passenger positions for use during multiplayer games when you want to load up your squad and take them into combat. For more information on the various types of vehicles in the game, see the Vehicles chapter, which is devoted entirely to vehicles.

★ MISSION INFORMATION ★

During combat, the side with the most information has the advantage. To gain some additional insight during a mission, press the menu button. During the single-player campaign, this also pauses the game. The menu screen contains some great assets. First off are the objectives. These include the overall objective as well as the current orders you must complete. Check in on your objectives and orders frequently to stay focused on the purpose and execution of your mission. Also on the menu screen is a larger map of the area in which you are operating. This is not only larger than the minimap, but it also shows a larger area. Use this map to determine which roads you need to take to get to a distant objective. This map uses the same symbols as the minimap and also shows all detected enemies as well as all friendlies. Use it to find enemies that are too far away to appear on your minimap.

TACTICS

Tactics is the combining of maneuvers and firepower to achieve an objective. Both movement and weapons have already been covered, so this section focuses on using the two together.

PLANNING AHEAD

Plan what you will do before you rush in.

There is an old saying that those who fail to plan, plan to fail. No matter whether you are playing the single-player campaign or multiplayer missions, you need to come up with a plan before the bullets start flying. The best place to start is to look at your objectives, since those determine victory or defeat. While killing the enemy is always a goal, it is often a means to an end. Instead, focus on the objectives. Do you have to destroy a target, defend a position, or just get to a certain point on the map.

Once you know what you must do, look at the map and examine the terrain. Where are you located? Where is the objective? How will you get there? Are there any vehicles you can use? These are all questions you need to ask yourself. Once you have determined how to get to the target, you must then consider how to accomplish your orders. If you need to destroy something, what weapons will you use? Will you need to get in close to plant an explosive charge on the target, or can you stay back and fire rockets at it? Finally, you need to take into account your opposition. What does the enemy have and where are they located? Usually you will not know that type of information until you get in close to the target and can see the enemy with your own eyes. Therefore, planning continues on the fly as you learn new information about enemy positions and actions.

USING COVER

Look for cover at all times. Even these metal plates along the catwalk will stop enemy fire from hitting you.

Combat is very dangerous. Bullets and other deadly projectiles fly through the air and can cause a lot of damage when they hit you. The concept of cover is to place something between you and the enemy that will stop those projectiles and keep you safe. The battlefields are filled with objects that you can use as cover—buildings, walls, trees, rocks, earthen mounds, and so on. Some types of cover will stop small arms fire such as rifle bullets, but not stop the heavier machine gun fire. Walls of buildings will stop machine gun fire, but not rockets or tank rounds. Therefore, pick a cover that will protect you from the current threat.

Cover should become ingrained in your combat thinking. In addition to looking for enemies, you also need to be looking for cover. During a fire fight, stay behind cover. The only reason you leave cover is to move to another position with cover. If the cover is low, you may need to crouch down behind it, standing only to fire over it. When moving from cover to cover, sprint to get there quicker.

While you want to stay behind cover, you also want to try to deny the benefits of cover to your enemies. Destroying their cover is a way to do that. Another way is to reduce the effect of their cover by moving to hit them from a direction in which they have no cover. This is called flanking. For example, if an enemy is taking cover behind a wall, move around to the side of the wall so that the wall is no longer between you and your target.

DESTRUCTIBLE ENVIRONMENT

Call in a mortar strike and destroy most of the building along with the enemies inside.

The topic of cover leads nicely into destructible environment. One of the awesome features in this game is that many of the structures and objects can be damaged or even destroyed. This presents a large range of possibilities and opportunities that will affect the tactics you use. For example, if the enemy is holed up in a house and taking shots at you from the windows, you could try to throw a grenade through the window or rush into the house via the doorway to clear the threat out with close-range combat. However, with destruction as an option, you can launch a grenade at a wall of the house and blow a hole in it. If an enemy was right on the other side, that threat might be killed. Otherwise, you can then use direct fire to kill the enemy, since you blew up the wall providing cover.

Often structures can funnel you into a kill zone the enemy has set up. Now you can blast your way through walls or other objects and come at the enemies from different directions that they might not expect. While this may seem to favor the attacker, the defender can also use this as an advantage. Destroy potential cover the attacker may use to approach your position. Call in mortar strikes on groves of trees or shoot out fences to deny the enemy a place to hide. As a result, you can create your own kill zones of open land which the enemy must traverse—all the while under the fire of your weapons.

★ TIP ★

Take some time practicing destroying objects and structures to get a feel for what weapons work against which targets. While you can blow off the exterior walls and roofs of buildings, interior walls can't be destroyed. Therefore, if you are hiding out in a building and the enemy has weapons that can destroy the exterior walls, take cover behind an interior wall. These will stop even tank rounds.

LONG-RANGE COMBAT

If possible, it is best to try to attack the enemy at long range before the enemy even knows you are there. While sniper rifles work great for this type of combat, you can even use assault rifles, light machine guns,

Snipe at enemies guarding a base to make it easier when you move in closer.

or rocket launchers to hit targets at long range. The key to winning at long range is to take your time. Crouch down, stay still, and use ironsights or scopes to increase your accuracy. As always, make sure you have some good cover in case the enemy decides to shoot back. Also remember to fire in short bursts to ensure that more of your bullets hit the target.

CLOSE-QUARTERS COMBAT

This type of combat is the exact opposite of long-range combat. In close quarters, such as in a town or even within a building, you don't have a lot of time to aim before shooting. However, at such short

You have to shoot fast when fighting in close quarters.

ranges, accuracy is not really a factor. Instead, you need a weapon that puts out a lot of firepower with some spread so you are more likely to get a hit while moving. Shotguns and submachine guns are great for close-quarters combat. Your minimap is also an important tool, since you can see where enemies are located and set up shots for strafing around a corner. Your weapon will already be aimed at the target as it appears on the minimap, which saves you just enough time to have the advantage and make the kill rather than be killed. Don't forget to use grenades, which can be thrown around corners or over walls to hit enemies who think they are safe behind cover.

ENGAGING FIXED WEAPONS POSITIONS

Try to hit fixed weapons positions from long range and from a flank.

There are three types of fixed weapons positions—machine guns, grenade launchers, and rocket launchers. Each must be manned by a soldier in order to be used. These weapons can be extremely deadly

during combat, so it is usually a top priority to silence these weapons either by destroying them outright or at least killing the soldiers firing them. Some machine guns and grenade launchers have a shield to protect the gunner. However, if you take careful aim, you can shoot through the vision slits in these shields to kill the gunner. Other options include using grenades or rockets to wipe out the weapon along with the gunner. Some of these weapons also have limited firing arcs and can't turn to fire at targets in all directions. If you can attack these guns from the flanks or sides, you can not only avoid being fired on by that weapon, but also possibly prevent the shield from protecting the gunner.

★ TIP ★

Try to silence fixed weapons positions at long range. Snipers work great for this job.

ENGAGING VEHICLES

Strafe out from behind cover to take your shot at a vehicle, then strafe back to reload.

Vehicles can be daunting during combat—especially when you are an infantryman on foot. However, modern soldiers have a lot of firepower they can use to destroy vehicles. This role usually falls to the demolitions class,

which carries anti-tank rocket launchers. It takes only a single rocket to destroy jeeps and armored jeeps. However, tanks and IFVs require two rocket hits for a kill. Other ways to destroy armored vehicles are by calling in a mortar strike or using the laser designator to guide a bomb right onto the top of the vehicle for a sure kill.

Even if you don't have those powerful weapons or gadgets, you can still stop jeeps and armored jeeps. The gunners on each of these vehicles are exposed. Shoot them, and the vehicles lose their firepower. For those who are really daring, support class soldiers

Of course the best way to destroy a tank is with another tank.

can place anti-tank mines in the path of moving vehicles and specialist class soldiers can place a C4 charge on a tank or other vehicle and detonate it. Only one charge is required to blow up a tank.

INFANTRY

As a member of Bad Company, you have the opportunity to use a variety of weapons and equipment. Some are issued at the start of each mission, others you can find on the battlefield in weapons caches or left behind by dead enemies. No two weapons are exactly the same, so get to know the weapons you will be using so you can select those that best reflect your style of combat.

★ PRIMARY WEAPONS ★

Primary weapons are the main weapons you use during combat. There are six different categories of primary weapons, each with their own specializations. When playing multiplayer games, you are limited to certain types of primary weapons, depending on your kit.

ASSAULT RIFLES

Assault rifles are the most versatile type of primary weapon. They are carried in the Assault kit and include an attached grenade launcher. Assault rifles are most effective at medium range; however, they can be used at close and long range as well. As such, they are the jack-of-all-trades on the battlefield. The grenade launcher gives some additional firepower and is useful for punching holes in walls or other types of cover. These rifle grenades detonate on impact and can kill nearby enemies caught within the blast radius.

NOTE ★★

For each weapon, a relative value is provided for the areas of Accuracy, Damage, and Rate of Fire, with 100 being the highest rating for each category. A rarity factor is also included for those weapons available in the single-player campaign.

AEK971

Accuracy: 70

Damage: 50

Rate of Fire: 60

Single-Player Frequency:
Common

Modern Russian assault rifle equipped with a recoil damper that enables stable handling during fully automatic fire. After years in development, the AEK971 is now the standard assault rifle of the Russian Army.

AN94

Accuracy: 80

Damage: 35

Rate of Fire: 80

Single-Player Frequency:
Uncommon

High-tech Russian rifle with an advanced firing mechanism that provides a very high rate of fire. Failed Army trials, but still remains a favorite among many special forces in Russia.

AUG

Accuracy: 70

Damage: 50

Rate of Fire: 60

Single-Player Frequency:
Rare

Battle-proven Austrian assault rifle widely known for its high performance and durability. Bullpup layout allows for a shorter stock while maintaining barrel length. Its aesthetic design has also made it a common sight in many Hollywood blockbusters.

F2000

Accuracy: 50

Damage: 20

Rate of Fire: 90

Single-Player Frequency:
Multiplayer only

Highly customizable Belgian assault rifle with a number of modification options, such as different scopes, grenade launcher attachments, computerized firing systems, and so on. The weapon has an ambidextrous fire selector, ejection port, and handle.

PRIMA Official Game Guide

BAD COMPANY
BATTLEFIELD

M16

Accuracy: 85

Damage: 60

Rate of Fire: 50

Single-Player Frequency:
Uncommon

The classic American work horse, having seen action all over the world for many decades. Its accuracy and handling are a true legacy of old American rifle traditions.

M416

Accuracy: 70

Damage: 50

Rate of Fire: 60

Single-Player Frequency:
Start of each mission

The M416 is an upgraded version of the M4 and M16 assault rifles. With new firing mechanics, this modification solved many of the performance issues with the old weapons systems, and also proved to be a more cost-effective solution than replacing the huge number of aging rifles in service.

XM8

Accuracy: 70

Damage: 40

Rate of Fire: 75

Single-Player Frequency:
Uncommon

Experimental U.S. weapons system based on the German G36 assault rifle. A highly accurate and dependable weapon with many "in the field" modification options. Despite its great performance, it never left the experimental phase.

SUBMACHINE GUNS

Submachine guns are designed for close-quarters combat. They are carried in the Specialist kit. Though they lack the range and accuracy of an assault rifle, their increased rate of fire makes them deadly up close. In addition, the submachine guns are equipped with a sound suppressor, which makes them very quiet. If you are using stealthy tactics to get to your objectives, then take along a submachine gun.

9A91

Accuracy: 50

Damage: 50

Rate of Fire: 90

Single-Player Frequency:
Rare

A Russian compact assault rifle chambered for special high-caliber ammunition. The steep trajectory and short sight base makes the rifle ineffective at long range, but up close it packs more stopping power than any other nine millimeter.

AKS74U

Accuracy: 50

Damage: 50

Rate of Fire: 90

Single-Player Frequency:
Common

A shortened, modified version of the legendary AK-47. Popular among Russian special forces for its size, but suffering from limited range and accuracy. Despite this, it's a very powerful and reliable rifle.

PP2000

Accuracy: 40

Damage: 30

Rate of Fire: 100

Single-Player Frequency:
Rare

Ultra modern Russian submachine gun, first shown to the public in 2004. Used by Russian police and security forces and claimed to be superior to many foreign competitors.

SCAR

Accuracy: 50

Damage: 50

Rate of Fire: 90

Single-Player Frequency:
Uncommon

The SCAR assault family consists of a heavy and light type, each available in several locations, with different barrel lengths and ammunition types. This light model is used by SOCOM forces and was accepted by them as late as 2003.

UMP

Accuracy: 60

Damage: 65

Rate of Fire: 60

Single-Player Frequency:
Rare

This German submachine gun was developed for the American law enforcement market. Very light weight and highly customizable.

XM8C

Accuracy: 60

Damage: 45

Rate of Fire: 70

Single-Player Frequency:
Rare

Compact version of the XM8 rifle. Very light weight and designed as a personal defense weapon.

UZI

Accuracy: 25

Damage: 50

Rate of Fire: 90

Single-Player Frequency:
Multiplayer only

Classic Israeli submachine gun. It has proven itself in countless countries during the last fifty years.

LIGHT MACHINE GUNS

Light machine guns are carried in the Support kit. They are designed to put out a high volume of fire that can cause a lot of damage. However, the down side is that light machine guns are less accurate than assault rifles and more difficult to handle. Use this type of weapon while crouched behind some type of cover to force the enemy to take cover. This way your squad mates can maneuver around or you, or your squad can mow down any enemy foolish enough to try to move out in the open.

M249

Accuracy: 55

Damage: 60

Rate of Fire: 60

Single-Player Frequency:
Rare

The standard U.S. Army light machine gun. Originally designed in Belgium, the rifle has a reputation of being extremely reliable and is widely used around the world by many armed forces.

MG3

Accuracy: 50

Damage: 35

Rate of Fire: 90

Single-Player Frequency:
Rare

An upgrade version of the classic WWII German MG42. The MG3 is capable of a very high rate of fire and, despite its age, this versatile and powerful machine gun is still in active service in many armies.

M60

Accuracy: 55

Damage: 50

Rate of Fire: 50

Single-Player Frequency:
Multiplayer only

Iconic American machine gun, famous for its service in the Vietnam war. Designed in the late 1940s, it borrows heavily from German WWII machine gun designs.

MG36

Accuracy: 70

Damage: 40

Rate of Fire: 75

Single-Player Frequency:
Uncommon

LMG version of the German Army G36 rifle. This modern rifle is equipped with a bipod, red point sights, and drum magazine for faster reloading.

PRIMA Official Game Guide

BATTLEFIELD BAD COMPANY

PKM

Accuracy: 55

Damage: 60

Rate of Fire: 60

Single-Player Frequency:
Common

Russian general-purpose machine gun. This high-caliber machine gun is famous for its power and reliability and is used in many different countries.

XM8 LMG

Accuracy: 50

Damage: 40

Rate of Fire: 75

Single-Player Frequency:
Uncommon

Squad automatic rifle (SAW) version of the XM8 rifle. Features a longer barrel, bipod, and dual drum magazine.

QJU88

Accuracy: 55

Damage: 60

Rate of Fire: 60

Single-Player Frequency:
Rare

The type 99 light machine gun is of Chinese origin and entered service in the PLA at the beginning of the 21st century.

SNIPER RIFLES

Designed for long-range combat, sniper rifles are carried in the Recon kit. Most of these weapons have a very low rate of fire since they are bolt action and require you to work the action after each shot. However, with their magnified scope view, you can kill enemies at great distances with a single hit. A few sniper rifles are semiautomatic, but fire smaller rounds, so you may need to get two or three hits for a kill. Due to their low rate of fire, it is best to stay at a distance from the enemy when carrying a sniper rifle.

NOTE ★★

Sniper rifles do not have a reticle in standard view. Therefore, they are difficult to use while moving around in close proximity to the enemy.

GOL

Accuracy: 100

Damage: 90

Rate of Fire: 5

Single-Player Frequency:
Rare

German bolt-action sniper rifle. This highly accurate and reliable rifle is available in a wide range of configurations and is currently used by several German police units as well as sporting groups around the world.

M24

Accuracy: 100

Damage: 90

Rate of Fire: 5

Single-Player Frequency:
Rare

Highly accurate sniper weapon system used by the U.S. military and police forces. The M24 uses the heaviest type of ammunition for this weapon class, providing very long range firing.

M95

Accuracy: 100

Damage: 100

Rate of Fire: 5

Single-Player Frequency:
Uncommon

A bolt-action version of the M82A1 weapon, with shorter total length thanks to the bullpup configuration. The large-caliber ammunition makes it a preferred sniper rifle for long-range sniping as well as anti-material tasks.

QBU88

Accuracy: 100

Damage: 85

Rate of Fire: 10

Single-Player Frequency:
Multiplayer only

Chinese marksman's rifle designed in the late 1980s. It features ironsights but is usually equipped with a 4x scope. Used by the PLA and Chinese police forces.

SV98

Accuracy: 100

Damage: 90

Rate of Fire: 5

Single-Player Frequency:
Common

An upgrade of the successful sporting rifle, this high-precision sniper rifle was built intentionally for domestic Russian use, such as the Spetznaz forces, counter-terrorist forces, and law enforcement groups. The weapon features a detachable scope and a special plastic magazine.

SVU

Accuracy: 90

Damage: 60

Rate of Fire: 30

Single-Player Frequency:
Rare

A bullpup version of the classic SVD design, this weapon is shorter and incorporates a suppressor. It can be used with its built-in ironsights, although the common setup features a scope. The SVU was designed with Russian law enforcement forces in mind.

VSS

Accuracy: 80

Damage: 50

Rate of Fire: 40

Single-Player Frequency:
Uncommon

A lightweight, short, and quiet sniper rifle using subsonic ammunition. It features a built-in sound suppressor, a wide array of scopes, and can be easily broken into three parts to allow discrete transportation. Despite its size, it fires a heavy round, which can penetrate a wide range of armor.

SHOTGUNS

Shotguns are one of two primary weapons carried in the Demolition kit. Like submachine guns, shotguns are good for close-quarters combat. However, the shotgun offers high damage at the cost of a low rate of fire. Shotguns will kill an enemy with a single shot and are still effective at close range without having to switch to ironsights view.

870MCS

Accuracy: 35

Damage: 80

Rate of Fire: 10

Single-Player Frequency:
Uncommon

Classic American shotgun. Modular Combat Shotgun (MCS) version. As the name implies, it allows the user to configure the weapon into different setups.

NS2000

Accuracy: 45

Damage: 80

Rate of Fire: 10

Single-Player Frequency:
Uncommon

South African pump-action shotgun featuring an unusual bullpup design for a shotgun. Another original solution is the magazine placement above the barrel. Also, in contrast to most pump-action shotguns, the pump action is forward.

S20K

Accuracy: 35

Damage: 50

Rate of Fire: 35

Single-Player Frequency:
Common

Standard shotgun of the Russian Ground Forces. This weapon has semi-automatic fire, allowing multiple shells to be fired in rapid succession. Uses a mechanism originally designed for assault rifles.

SPAS12

Accuracy: 25

Damage: 80

Rate of Fire: 10

Single-Player Frequency:
Rare

Legendary Italian combat shotgun with iconic folding stock. Manufacture stopped in 2000.

PRIMA Official Game Guide

BAD COMPANY
BATTLEFIELD

SPAS15

Accuracy: 25

Damage: 55

Rate of Fire: 30

Single-Player Frequency:
Rare

Modern semi-automatic shotgun featuring a standard box magazine that allows for much faster loading compared to standard tubular magazines, where the shells need to be loaded one by one.

USA12

Accuracy: 40

Damage: 60

Rate of Fire: 30

Single-Player Frequency:
Multiplayer only

Gas-operated South Korean combat shotgun capable of fully automatic 12-gauge fire. Bulky, heavy, and powerful, this massive rifle is banned from civilian use in the U.S.

TT94

Accuracy: 35

Damage: 80

Rate of Fire: 10

Single-Player Frequency:
Rare

Russian 12-gauge pump-action shotgun. Not used by Russian armed forces, but successfully exported to international buyers.

ROCKET LAUNCHERS

Demolition kits also carry a rocket launcher along with their shotgun. In the single-player campaign, rocket launchers are treated as a secondary weapon that you can carry in lieu of an item. Rocket launchers are primarily designed for destroying enemy vehicles. However, they can also be used to punch holes in structures or to demolish cover. Rocket launchers feature a scope, allowing for greater accuracy at longer distances.

M2CG

M136

RPG7

Each nationality features their own type of infantry anti-tank system. However, within the game, they all function the same way.

In addition to a primary weapon, you can also carry additional items to help you complete your objectives.

ATM-00 ANTI-TANK MINE

The anti-tank mine is only available during multiplayer games and is carried in the Demolition kit. This explosive is placed on the ground, preferably in the location through which enemy vehicles travel. It is automatically armed when put down and detonates when a vehicle drives over it. This works well in conjunction with a rocket launcher for vehicle ambushes set up along a road or other well-traveled route.

COMBAT KNIFE

Every soldier is equipped with a combat knife. Press the knife button to quickly unsheathe this weapon and make an attack. The knife comes in handy when  close to an enemy, if you need to reload, or are completely out of ammo. You can also use the combat knife to break down wooden doors or fences.

DTN-4

This item is actually two different items that work together. The first is C4 plastic explosive with a radio detonator inserted into it. You can place this explosive charge on the ground, on items, or even on vehicles. Once the first charge has been set, you automatically switch to the remote detonator. Press the fire button to blow the charge. You can also set several charges and then blow them up all at once. Just follow the on-screen directions.

TIP

In addition to blowing up structures such as walls or bridges, you can also blow up vehicles, including tanks, by placing a DTN-4 on the vehicle and then detonating it from a safe distance. These explosives can even be used for ambushes. Place in an area where the enemy will not see it and then wait to detonate it until the enemy is next to the explosive. This item is available to the Specialist kit once unlocked after leveling up.

HAND GRENADE

All classes except for assault and recon carry hand grenades with them. Once selected, throw grenades by pressing the fire button. The longer you hold the button down before releasing, the farther your grenade goes. Hand grenades are great for throwing around corners, through windows, or over cover.

LIFE-2

This is a chemical dispenser for emergency treatment in the field. One use restores your health to 100 percent. It can be used over and over again, though it takes a few seconds to recharge after each use. During the single-player campaign, you have this item with you at all times. However, during multiplayer games, it is available only in the Assault kit after it has been unlocked by leveling up.

LZ-537

Upon successfully targeting an enemy vehicle, a laser-guided bomb will be released at high altitude. This bomb can be controlled remotely by the user. Since you can steer the bomb, you do not have to guide it to the targeted vehicle. Instead, you can steer it to a structure or even a fixed weapon position that you would not be able to initially target. Recon kits gain access to this item after leveling up.

Welcome • Basic Training • Infantry • Vehicles • Campaign • Multiplayer • Appendix

Welcome to Bad Company | Acta non Verba | Crossing Over | Par for the Course | Air Force One | Crash and Grab | Ghost Town

MEDIC KITS

The medic kit is a part of the Support kit. It allows a soldier to not only heal him or herself, but also to heal others. The medic kit can be held to quickly heal others or dropped for others to pick up.

MOTION SENSOR

The motion sensor is part of the Recon kit. It is a small ball-shaped object that can be thrown like a grenade. However, once it lands and activates, it reveals all enemies within a small radius of the sensor. Check your minimap to see where they are located. The motion sensor operates for a limited amount of time. Try throwing it next to a building to see if there are any enemies inside.

MRTR-5

A GPS transmitter, directly linked to allied mortar arrays. This fully automated system allows for immediate artillery support when it's most needed. This item is unlocked once a soldier with the Support kit levels up. Unlike the LZ-537 laser designator, the MRTR-5 can be used on any type of target. Use it to destroy buildings and bridges, and even clear out forests. The mortar barrage can destroy vehicles, though tanks usually require a couple barrages before they are eliminated.

PISTOL

Since the Recon kit's sniper rifles are not very good at close-range combat, this kit includes a pistol instead of hand grenades. While each nationality has their own type of pistol, all function similarly. They are semi-automatic and it takes a few hits to bring down an enemy—unless you get a head shot which does the job with a single hit.

POWER TOOL

The power tool is another item included in the Support kit. Soldiers can use the power tool to fix vehicles. Select the power tool as your current item and then hold down the fire button while standing next to a vehicle to begin repairing it.

TRACER GUN

If you are playing with the Specialist kit, you come equipped with a tracer gun. Fire this gun at a vehicle to "tag" the vehicle for demolition class soldiers on your team. When they look through the scope view of their rocket launcher, they are able to get a lock on the vehicle. When they fire, the missile will home in on the tracer dart and score a hit on the vehicle. This makes hitting a moving vehicle much easier.

★ FIXED WEAPONS ★

In addition to the weapons you carry on your person, you can also find fixed weapons on the maps. These powerful weapons have unlimited ammo, but cannot be moved. They are great for defending a position against enemy attack.

MACHINE GUN

The machine gun is excellent for defending against enemy infantry. While it has unlimited ammo, you can't fire it non-stop. As you fire it, the machine gun heats up, and once the heat meter at the bottom right is empty, the gun stops firing until it cools down. Since the machine gun automatically cools when you are not firing, fire this weapon in short bursts rather than long, continuous streams of lead. This keeps your gun from overheating, which can be very bad during the middle of an attack. Some machine guns feature a protective shield and all have a limited arc through which they can fire, so watch out for enemies approaching on your flanks.

GRENADE LAUNCHER

The grenade launcher is a wonderful weapon for attacking infantry as well as light vehicles. It launches grenades automatically as long as you hold down the fire button. However, like the machine gun, it overheats and stops firing unless you let it cool down. The grenade launcher heats up very quickly, so shoot in short bursts to prolong your ability to fire.

ROCKET LAUNCHER

The rocket launcher fires anti-tank rockets that can travel 360 degrees. After firing a rocket, you can continue to guide it by keeping the reticle centered on the target. This allows you to easily hit moving targets as long as they remain within your line of sight. After each shot, you must wait for the launcher to reload a rocket before you can fire again. You can also use this weapon to blow holes in buildings and other structures. If you want to take out a bridge, shoot out over the bridge and then guide it down onto the bridge to knock out a section.

ANTI-AIRCRAFT GUN

This weapon works well for shooting down enemy helicopters. The anti-aircraft gun fires exploding rounds that can also be used against ground vehicles and even infantry. Like other fixed weapons, the anti-aircraft gun can overheat when fired continuously, so limit yourself to bursts.

ARTILLERY

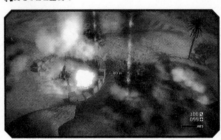

Artillery is a very powerful fixed weapon. Once you take control of this gun, you select your targets using an aerial view of the battlefield from a drone. Once you know what you want to bombard, press the fire button and watch the fireworks. The down side to artillery is that the area in which you can attack is limited. However, your bombardments destroy structures, vehicles, and any infantry unlucky enough to get caught in it.

★ KITS ★

When playing *Battlefield: Bad Company* multiplayer games, you must select a kit for your soldier. A kit is a selection of weapons and equipment for a specific class of soldier. Within each kit, you may be able to select your primary weapon. However, the other weapons and items are set. Due to the differences in the kits, it is important to know the strengths and limitations of each kit so that you can successfully play your role during a battle. Let's look at the five kits.

ASSAULT KIT

> **ASSAULT RIFLE WITH GRENADE LAUNCHER**
>
> **LIFE-2 INJECTOR (UNLOCKABLE)**
>
> **COMBAT KNIFE**

The Assault kit is the standard vanilla kit. It is good for engaging enemy infantry at close to medium range. It lacks any major firepower for dealing with vehicles, but the attached grenade launcher gives assault soldiers the ability to bust through walls and cover. Once the Life-2 injector is unlocked, assault soldiers can heal themselves, thus allowing them to stay on the battlefield much longer. For new players, this is the kit with which to start.

DEMOLITION KIT

> **SHOTGUN**
>
> **ROCKET LAUNCHER**
>
> **HAND GRENADES**
>
> **ANTI-TANK MINES (UNLOCKABLE)**
>
> **COMBAT KNIFE**

The Demolition kit is much more specialized. Its main focus is to eliminate enemy vehicles with the rocket launcher and anti-tank mines. However, this class can also be useful for destroying defensive positions. While moving around the battlefield, have your shotgun ready rather than your rocket launcher to quickly neutralize enemy infantry you come across. Since the shotgun is a short-range weapon, demolition class soldiers are good for urban warfare where the combat is in close quarters.

PRIMA Official Game Guide

Welcome · Basic Training · Infantry · Vehicles · Campaign · Multiplayer · Appendix

Welcome to Bad Company | Acta non Verba | Crossing Over | Par for the Course | Air Force One | Crash and Grab | Ghost Town

RECON KIT

- SNIPER RIFLE
- PISTOL
- MOTION SENSOR
- L2-537 LASER DESIGNATOR (UNLOCKABLE)
- COMBAT KNIFE

The Recon kit is designed to engage the enemy at long range. Both the sniper rifle and the laser designator give recon class soldiers very effective ways to fight against both infantry and vehicles at long range. As a result, they are poor for fighting against enemies at close range. While on the move, keep your pistol out and ready, since it is difficult to fire a sniper rifle with any accuracy from the hip—plus you do not have a reticle when you are not looking through the scope. Use the motion sensor to help prevent enemies from sneaking up on you while you are focusing your attention through the scope.

SPECIALIST KIT

- SUBMACHINE GUN
- TRACER GUN
- HAND GRENADES
- DTN-4 EXPLOSIVES (UNLOCKABLE)
- COMBAT KNIFE

The Specialist kit is great for urban warfare. Armed with a submachine gun complete with a sound suppressor, specialist class soldiers can move in for quick and quiet kills without alerting nearby enemies to their presence. Since they are good for getting in close, use the tracer gun to tag vehicles so demolition class soldiers at medium to long range can effectively engage enemy vehicles. As soon as specialist class soldiers rank up, they can use the explosive charges. These can destroy structures such as buildings and bridges, and even be placed on vehicles. In fact, if you can sneak into the enemy base, place explosive charges on empty vehicles and then detonate them once an enemy soldier hops in to drive away.

SUPPORT KIT

- LIGHT MACHINE GUN
- HAND GRENADES
- POWER TOOL
- MRTR-5 MORTAR STRIKE (UNLOCKABLE)
- COMBAT KNIFE

Every team needs some soldiers with the Support kit. Support soldiers should try to stay at medium range from the enemy since they can't move or reload their weapon as quickly as other kits. The light machine gun gives support class soldiers some heavy firepower, which is great for covering an area when on the defense or for clearing out defenses while on the attack. When playing as support, watch the minimap for yellow crosses and wrenches. These show the locations of friendly soldiers in need of healing as well as vehicles in need of repair. You can earn a lot of points towards leveling up by healing and repairing, plus you can even heal yourself. Once you level up, the mortar strike capability is awesome—especially when you are the attacker and want to clear out a section of enemy defenses.

THE MOTOR POOL

One of the highlights of any *Battlefield* game is the vehicles. Nothing can be more entertaining than hopping into a main battle tank and cruising across the landscape, laying waste to both enemy vehicles and structures alike. *Battlefield: Bad Company* continues this tradition and lets you climb into tanks, jeeps, helicopters, and even boats to quickly move across the battlefield with lots of firepower.

TANKS

Tanks are the heavy hitters on the battlefield. They are armed with a large-caliber cannon as well as a machine gun. They have the heaviest armor of any vehicle and can take several hits before they are destroyed. There are four seats in a tank. The driver also mans the main gun. The gunner controls the machine gun mounted on top of the turret. There are also two passenger seats. Tanks operate best out in the open where they can use their long-range firepower to engage enemy vehicles and infantry. Urban warfare is a challenge for tanks since enemy infantry can use buildings for cover and get in close to attack. Tanks are equipped with smoke mortars that instantly create a temporary smokescreen around the tank in all directions, allowing you to avoid incoming fire and make repairs when natural cover is not available.

PRIMA Official Game Guide

BAD COMPANY
BATTLEFIELD

★ INFANTRY FIGHTING VEHICLES ★

Infantry fighting vehicles (IFV) are essentially light tanks. They lack the heavy armor of the tank, but still have a lot of firepower. Their main weapon is an auto cannon, which fires high-explosive rounds in quick succession as long as you hold down the fire button. Like other rapid-fire weapons, the auto cannon will overheat, so fire in quick bursts. The IFV also has a machine gun on its turret. The driver controls the auto cannon while the gunner mans the machine gun. There are also two passenger seats. IFVs are great for engaging any type of vehicle, except for a tank.

ANTI-AIRCRAFT VEHICLES

Anti-aircraft vehicles are essentially an IFV chassis with an anti-aircraft gun mounted in place of a turret. The driver only drives the vehicle while the gunner position mans the anti-aircraft gun. This vehicle is deadly to enemy helicopters and can also be used to attack light vehicles and infantry. The gunner is exposed and can be killed by small arms fire.

PRIMA Official Game Guide

BATTLEFIELD BAD COMPANY

★ ARMORED JEEPS ★

Armored jeeps have some armor and are armed with a machine gun in an open turret. These vehicles are faster than tanks or IFVs, but lack the same amount of protective armor. As a result, armored jeeps can be destroyed with a single shot from a rocket launcher or even from sustained machine gun fire. The driver only drives the vehicle. The gunner has a shield to the front, but is exposed from other directions. There are also two passenger seats.

LIGHT JEEPS

The light jeep trades armor for speed and firepower. All soldiers riding in a light jeep are exposed to enemy fire. However, the light jeep is fast and armed with a grenade launcher in a turret as well as a machine gun, which can fire within a forward facing arc. The driver focuses on driving while two gunner positions can put out a lot of firepower. There is also a single passenger seat.

TRUCKS

Trucks are your last choice for transportation. They lack any armor or weapons and are slower than the armored jeeps. In addition to a driver, a truck can carry three passengers.

PRIMA Official Game Guide

BAD COMPANY

BATTLEFIELD

★ HELICOPTERS ★

Helicopters allow you to cross the battlefield quickly without regards to terrain. The pilot not only does the flying, but also can fire volleys of rockets that are effective against vehicles, infantry, and even structures. The gunner mans a chaingun in a chin turret, which is good for attacking infantry and vehicles. Helicopters are vulnerable to anti-aircraft gun fire as well as rocket launchers. When piloting a helicopter, keep it moving so it is more difficult for the enemy to try and shoot you down.

Boats are a quick method of travelling a map's waterways. Though the crew are exposed, the boat has a lot of firepower. The driver only controls the movement of the boat. One gunner mans a forward grenade launcher with a limited firing arc while a second gunner is at the rear grenade launcher. The boat can also carry a single passenger. Boats are not armored and can easily be sunk if you are not careful. Your best defense is to keep the boat moving at high speed so it is very difficult for the enemy to hit you with rocket launcher fire.

When using a vehicle, it is always a good idea for one of the crew to be a support class soldier. Therefore, when the vehicle takes damage, the support class soldier can repair it using the power tool.

PRIMA Official Game Guide

BAD COMPANY
BATTLEFIELD

Welcome · Basic Training · Infantry · Vehicles · Campaign · Multiplayer · Appendix

Welcome to Bad Company | Acta non Verba | Crossing Over | Par for the Course | Air Force One | Crash and Grab | Ghost Town

WELCOME TO BAD COMPANY

The name is Preston Marlowe. I have been assigned to the 222nd Infantry. As the chopper dropped me off with my new squad, I had a lot of apprehension. Sarge seems like the only one who knows what he is doing and is not a screw-up. Sweetwater is the squad support and carries a light machine gun. I am told he is good at electronics, but some of his opinions are really out there. Haggard is our demolition man. His rocket launcher will probably come in handy. However, I have this fear that his fascination with blowing things up—and his impulsiveness—is going to get me into more trouble. As if it can get any worse than Bad Company.

Collectibles in this mission: 5
Gold in this mission: 0

After making introductions, we got the orders to move out. That didn't take long. Bad Company is usually assigned the lead position during operations. While being the point of the spear may sound glamorous and exciting, all that first to fight crap, the point also gets dulled quickly, or even broken. We climbed aboard a truck and started driving toward the front lines. Shortly thereafter, the convoy came under enemy fire. As we engaged in retrograde movement—that's Army speak for heading away from the enemy—our truck took a hit and I was knocked unconscious.

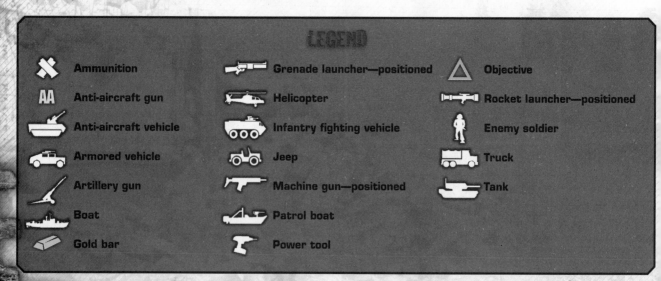

LEGEND

Ammunition	Grenade launcher—positioned	Objective
Anti-aircraft gun	Helicopter	Rocket launcher—positioned
Anti-aircraft vehicle	Infantry fighting vehicle	Enemy soldier
Armored vehicle	Jeep	Truck
Artillery gun	Machine gun—positioned	Tank
Boat	Patrol boat	
Gold bar	Power tool	

primagames.com

REACH SWEETWATER ⏺ DESTROY THE BARRELS ⏺ FILL UP ON AMMO ⏺ BLOW A HOLE IN THE HOUSE
FIND A POWER TOOL ⏺ REPAIR THE VEHICLE

Collectibles in this area: 0
Gold in this area: 0

Sarge tells you to look up and down.

Upon regaining consciousness, you see that you survived the attack that destroyed your truck and left you in a ditch. Before moving, Sarge wants to make sure that you are alright. Follow the onscreen directions to look up and then look down. If you like the control scheme, press the button next to "Controls are Good". If you prefer to invert the controls for looking up and down, press the button next to "Invert Controls".

REACH SWEETWATER

You now receive your first order—reach Sweetwater. The minimap enlarges when you receive a new order or objective. A red triangle designates the objective location on the minimap. A

Jump up onto this rock.

red triangle also appears in your HUD making it easier to see your objective without looking at the minimap. Walk forward along the bottom of the ditch until you come to a rock in your path. Continue to move forward, press the jump button to hop up onto the rock, and continue on.

As you continue down the ditch toward Sweetwater, your path will eventually be blocked by a wrecked automobile. To get past this obstacle, you need to crouch

Duck under this car.

down. Press the crouch button, then walk under the car to get to the other side. Press the crouch button again to stand back up. Keep walking until you reach Sweetwater.

If you look at your health level in the lower-right corner of the screen, you'll notice you are at only 50 health. Get it back up to 100. Press the cycle gadgets button once to bring up your auto injector.

The auto injector heals you.

No matter how low your health, one injection from this brings you back up to 100 health. Press the fire button to use the injector.

PRIMA Official Game Guide

BAD COMPANY
BATTLEFIELD

Welcome · Basic Training · Infantry · Vehicles · Campaign · Multiplayer · Appendix

Welcome to Bad Company | Acta non Verba | Crossing Over | Par for the Course | Air Force One | Crash and Grab | Ghost Town

TIP

After using the auto injector, it must recharge before you can use it again. A recharge meter appears below your current health level and illustrates the recharge process. It takes about ten seconds to recharge the auto injector. During combat, stay safe until the auto injector is ready before rushing into enemy fire.

DESTROY THE BARRELS

Now that you are back up to full health, press the cycle weapons button to bring up your assault rifle. Your new order is to destroy three barrels located in front of a nearby building. Throughout the

Destroy the three explosive barrels.

game, you will find similar barrels. Since they contain a highly volatile substance, they will blow up when you shoot them, killing nearby enemies and damaging adjacent structures or objects. It doesn't matter which barrel you shoot first. Target the barrel with the aiming reticle and press the fire button. The barrel disappears in a cloud of flames after a couple rounds hit it.

For the next barrel, hold down the zoom button to bring up the ironsights view. The aiming reticule disappears and is replaced by a view of you looking down the barrel of the rifle, using

Ironsights are best for medium- to long-range shots where increased accuracy is necessary.

the weapon's sights for aiming. Ironsights decreases your peripheral vision, but increases your accuracy. Line up a barrel with your ironsights and fire. Destroy the third barrel to complete this objective.

FILL UP ON AMMO

Reload and pick up more ammo at the ammo box.

Good job. Now change the magazine in your weapon by pressing the reload button. It is always a good idea to keep your weapon fully loaded. Since you do not lose any ammo when you reload, always top off your weapon so you are ready to fight when an enemy appears. It is dangerous to get into a fire fight with only a few rounds left in your magazine, so after each engagement, reload. Your new objective is to fill up on ammo. An ammo box is located next to the fence in front of the building. A red triangle appears over the box to show that it is your next objective. Picking up ammo is very easy. Just walk up to the ammo box, and your available ammo is restored to its maximum amount. However, this will not top off your magazine. You still need to reload for that.

TIP

Whenever you use an ammo box, the available ammo for all of your weapons is restored—even your weapons not currently in hand. For example, if you are holding your rifle, your grenades, rockets, and so forth are also maxed out.

BLOW A HOLE IN THE HOUSE

Use this house for target practice.

Continuing the tutorial, your next objective is to blow a hole in the house. Use your grenade launcher which is attached to your assault rifle. Press the cycle weapons button to activate your grenade launcher. Notice that your aiming reticle changes. Since grenades do not have a high muzzle velocity like that of a bullet, they fly through the air in an arc. Therefore, the more distant your target, the higher you must aim to lob the grenade right where you want it to hit. Grenades fired from a launcher detonate on impact which makes them very effective for destroying structures. Fire a grenade at the house and watch the destruction.

Take this opportunity to get a feel for the range of your grenade launcher. You carry eight grenades—however, if you run out, just walk over to the ammo box for a refill. While the objective is just to

The same house—about a dozen grenades later.

blow a hole in the house, fire a lot of grenades to completely destroy the house. You can't cause the house to collapse or destroy interior walls, but you can take out all the exterior walls and the roof.

Entering a building occupied by enemies can be very dangerous. Grenades and other explosives give you another option. Blow holes in the walls to expose hiding enemies as well as to create new entrances so you can avoid the doorways. Also, since interior walls can't be destroyed, fire grenades at them when an enemy is nearby. The grenade detonates on the wall and the resulting explosion kills the enemy.

FIND A POWER TOOL

Your next objective is located inside the building. Walk in the house through a hole you created and pick up the power tool. This item is considered a gadget and can be accessed by pressing the cycle gadgets button. However, when you pick it up, it becomes your active item.

Weapons crates often have weapons or equipment on top of them for you to take.

REPAIR THE VEHICLE

Fix this ride. You will need to use it to get to your next objective.

A nearby vehicle is in need of repair. Walk over to the armored jeep with your power tool in hand. Once you are next to the vehicle, press the fire button to begin repairing it. The reticle of the power tool shows how much damage the vehicle has sustained. As you repair, the crescent shaped bar begins to fill up. When it is completely full, the vehicle is fully repaired. It is very handy to have a power tool available when using vehicles.

★ STOP THE ARTILLERY SHELLING ★

LOCATE AND ELIMINATE THE ARTILLERY CREWS.

➤ ELIMINATE ARTILLERY CREWS ➤ REGROUP AT THE SMOKE

Now that you are comfortable with moving around and using weapons and equipment, it is time to put your training to use. Enemy artillery positions to the east are bombarding U.S. troops. Your squad has been assigned to halt the shelling by taking out the enemy manning the guns.

Drive to the east along the road until you come to these vehicle barriers.

AEK971

$20K ON SOLDIERS IN BUILDINGS

Collectibles in this area: 2
Gold in this area: 0

BAD COMPANY BATTLEFIELD

PRIMA Official Game Guide

Welcome • Basic Training • Infantry • Vehicles • Campaign • Multiplayer • Appendix

Welcome to Bad Company | Acta non Verba | Crossing Over | Par for the Course | Air Force One | Crash and Grab | Ghost Town

While standing next to the humvee, press the button shown at the bottom of the screen to enter the vehicle. You automatically take the driver's position and the rest of your squad climbs aboard with no further effort. Press the accelerate button to get moving. Follow the dirt road all the way to the end and disembark.

ELIMINATE ARTILLERY CREWS

Walk into the building near the large radio antenna. From the northern window, look down on two houses below. A single soldier patrols in front of the houses. Bring up the ironsights and take aim at

Line up a shot on the enemy soldier patrolling below.

him. While this is a long range shot for an assault rifle, you can still kill the enemy. Fire a couple quick bursts to drop him. There are two more soldiers down below—one in each of the houses. However, you can't get both of them from this vantage point. Exit the building and stop by the ammo box to top off after reloading your rifle.

The second soldier is located toward the back of this house.

Advance to the stone wall to the north of the antenna. While using the wall for cover, fire at the explosive barrel to the left of the door of the house directly ahead of you. When the barrel blows up, it takes out a

chunk of the house's wall. You may need to launch a grenade at the wall of the house around the door to expose the enemy inside. He is usually in the center of the house. Once you can see him, either shoot him directly, or fire at the artillery shells positioned along the back wall of the house. The resulting explosion kills the soldier and takes out the back wall of the house.

Shoot these barrels to punch a hole in the corner of the second house.

Now fire at the explosive barrels near the house to the right. This will usually expose the third soldier if you can fire at him quickly. If you can't see him through the hole, launch a grenade at the wall section to the right of the hole. The key is to kill the soldiers in the area at a distance and

without coming under fire yourself. On the chance that you can't get this last soldier from your position behind the wall, you will have to advance on the house and shoot him at closer range. However, before you head down to the houses, make a quick trip back to the ammo box to stock up on bullets and grenades since the next ammo box is in the middle of your objectives.

You can pick up the weapons dropped by the dead soldiers.

Head down the hill to the houses you have cleared. Dead enemies leave behind their weapons. The soldier that was patrolling outside of the houses drops an AEK971 assault rifle which is very similar to your own

M416. The enemies in the houses have S20K semiautomatic shotguns. While you are best keeping your assault rifle, pick up one of each of the enemy weapons to unlock them as collectibles, then pick your M416 back up again. You only need to pick up a weapon to have it credited to your collectible tally. You don't have to carry it or use it.

Watch for enemies coming down the trail.

It is now time to move on toward the objectives. Advance through the house on the left and out the back door—or hole—and take cover behind some sandbags. A couple soldiers advance toward you one at a time.

As soon as you can see them, fire and take them down.

★ TIP ★

If you take some damage during this fire fight, heal yourself with the auto injector as soon as it is over. It is a good habit to use this item as soon as you take damage during combat. Be sure to get behind some cover and the process only takes a couple seconds. As soon as you use the auto injector, quickly press the cycle weapons button to bring your rifle back up and ready to fire.

Advance toward the first artillery gun cautiously and be ready to fire.

There are three soldiers at each gun. After killing two soldiers along the trail, there is only one left near the first artillery gun. Reload your rifle if necessary and then crouch down and begin moving toward this first objective. As you approach, look for a head rising above the sandbags or watch for enemy fire. Be ready to shoot quickly to kill the enemy and clear the first gun.

Before continuing down the trail, enter the area around the first gun and take cover behind the sandbags. From this position, you can see the second artillery gun. Notice the red crate near this objective.

Shoot the red crate so the explosion takes out some of the enemies near the second gun.

Shooting it causes it to explode and kill some of the nearby enemies. Also try launching a few grenades at the position to remove the sandbags that the enemy might be using for cover or to destroy the enemies outright. From the first artillery gun, you can usually take down two of the three soldiers at the second gun.

Crouch down and advance along the trail toward the second artillery gun. Keep an eye on the minimap to see where the remaining enemy soldier is located. Sometimes, if he is behind a sandbag, you can take a shot at his

Stop by this ammo box after clearing the second gun.

exposed head. Don't be afraid to use grenades. As soon as you clear this artillery gun, restock all of your ammo at the ammo box along the trail across from the second objective.

Stay crouched as you advance. Watch for the exposed heads of your enemies and try to kill them before they can fire at you.

One more artillery gun remains to be cleared. As before, take cover behind the sandbags at this artillery position and try to shoot as many enemies ahead of you before advancing. Usually one or two soldiers from the last gun will advance toward you. Drop them in their tracks. Now crouch down and begin moving toward your objective. While only one soldier should be near the artillery gun, a few more will approach along the trail ahead of you. Be ready to take them out when they arrive. To help clear the last artillery position, shoot the red crate on the left side to blow out a section of sandbags and possibly kill the soldier on the other side.

REGROUP AT THE SMOKE

Red smoke often appears at the end of a main objective.

Once all three artillery guns have been cleared, you receive a new order—regroup at the smoke. Move to this location where the rest of your squad is waiting to receive a new objective.

PRIMA Official Game Guide

BATTLEFIELD BAD COMPANY

Welcome · Basic Training · Infantry · Vehicles · Campaign · Multiplayer · Appendix

Welcome to Bad Company | Acta non Verba | Crossing Over | Par for the Course | Air Force One | Crash and Grab | Ghost Town

PROTECT THE CONVOY

USE THE ENEMY ARTILLERY TO STOP AN ATTACK ON ALLIED TROOPS.

▸ MAN THE ARTILLERY GUN   ▸ SHELL THE INCOMING VEHICLES

MAN THE ARTILLERY GUN

Friendly troops near where you did your tutorial are under attack from enemy vehicles and infantry. Your squad has been ordered to use the artillery you just cleared to engage the enemy

Time to fire the big gun.

and protect the U.S. convoy. As the new guy, you get the honor of doing the shooting—and the blame if you hit friendly troops. Walk up to the artillery gun you cleared last and take control of it just like you would enter a vehicle.

SHELL THE INCOMING VEHICLES

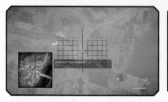

Take aim, fire, and watch the fireworks.

As soon as you are on the artillery gun, your view switches to a targeting screen, giving you an overhead view of the battle area. Enemy vehicles are driving toward the convoy. Since it takes a few seconds for your rounds to hit the target area, while the vehicles are moving, target a position along the road in front of them. It takes some time for the gun to reload, so by the time you can fire again, the vehicles will have come to a halt. Place the crosshairs over remaining vehicles and fire to destroy them. There is a total of three waves of vehicles to destroy to complete this objective.

OBJECTIVE RAM

SECURE AN ALTERNATE ROUTE FOR THE U.S. SUPPLY CONVOY.

▸ PROCEED TOWARD THE RIVER CROSSING   ▸ SEARCH THE HOUSE FOR A WEAPON   ▸ ELIMINATE ALL ENEMIES   ▸ REGROUP AT THE SMOKE

PROCEED TOWARD THE RIVER CROSSING

Head back to the road.

The bridge across the river near the convoy had been destroyed. Your new objective is to secure another crossing so the convoy can continue. Continue down the trail and hop down from a ledge to follow the trail back to the road where a humvee is waiting.

Collectibles in this area: 1
Gold in this area: 0

Since you don't need the enemy's vehicle, you can destroy it. Once you get to the road, sprint to the humvee and climb in. Then press the switch seat button to man the machine gun. Fire at the enemy vehicle with a long sustained burst until it is destroyed. Then finish off any surviving infantry.

The humvee's machine gun makes short work of the enemy vehicle.

If you want to destroy the enemy vehicle while on foot, launch grenades at it. Since it takes about five hits to destroy the vehicle, this option takes longer. However, it is the type of attack Haggard would approve.

Drive past the house you blew a hole in during training.

Climb into the humvee. Drive your squad back down the road. Pass through the area where you did some training as well as the remains of the vehicles destroyed with your artillery barrages. Drive around the wrecks, past the convoy, and on toward the next river crossing. As you approach a house, you get a new order to search this building.

SEARCH THE HOUSE FOR A WEAPON

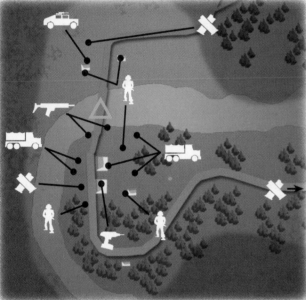

Break down the door with your knife, then pick up a new weapon.

An enemy vehicle approaches. Open fire!

As you get to the road, an enemy vehicle drives up and begins attacking your squad. When it comes to a stop, a soldier jumps out while another continues to man the vehicle's machine gun. Fire at the gunner since he is the biggest threat as you take cover behind the humvee. Then finish off the dismounted soldier. You now have your choice of taking the enemy vehicle or the humvee. Use your power tool to repair any damage either vehicle may have sustained during the fire fight.

PRIMA Official Game Guide

BAD COMPANY
BATTLEFIELD

Welcome · Basic Training · Infantry · Vehicles · Campaign · Multiplayer · Appendix

Welcome to Bad Company | Acta non Verba | Crossing Over | Par for the Course | Air Force One | Crash and Grab | Ghost Town

Stop in front of the house and disembark from your vehicle. The door is closed. Instead of blowing a hole in the house, press the knife button to use your knife to break down the door. Enter the house and locate some weapons cases. On top of them sits an XM8 assault rifle. Pick it up to unlock another collectible and keep this weapon to use for the mission. With your new toy in hand, climb back into your vehicle and continue down the road.

Man one of the machine guns by the river and stop the enemy counterattack.

ELIMINATE ALL ENEMIES

Snipe at the soldiers below.

Your next orders are to eliminate all of the enemies at the river crossing. They have set up a base here and you must clear it out. There are a couple of ways to go about this. The first is to try to take out as many soldiers as possible at a distance before rushing into the base. To do this, halt your vehicle near the wooden fence where the road takes a turn toward the south. From this vantage point, you can see soldiers patrolling the base down below. Use your ironsights for more accuracy during these long-range shots. Also shoot at explosive barrels and crates to add to the mayhem. Once you have cleared out as many enemies as you can, rush down the hill to continue clearing out the base.

As soon as you have cleared the enemy base, more troops counterattack from the opposite side of the river. Rush to one of the two machine guns and man it while Sweetwater or another squad mate mans the other. Soldiers located in the two wooden structures across the river fire on you. Take them out as well as the infantry rushing down the road and crossing the river. Fire in bursts rather than holding down the trigger for constant fire. This prevents your machine gun from overheating. Keep an eye on the heat meter located in the lower-right corner below your health counter.

Just as you finish off the last of the infantry, an enemy armored vehicle begins crossing the river and firing on your position. Your machine gun can't hurt this beast. However, stay put, healing

The enemy sends in an IFV.

yourself if necessary, and wait for support to arrive. A friendly helicopter gunship flies in to destroy the vehicle. It looks like the cavalry really did come to the rescue.

Use the vehicle machine gun to mow down enemies.

The other option is to stay in the humvee and continue driving right up to the entrance to the base. Rather than crashing through the gate, stop at the entrance and switch seats to man the machine gun. Fire at enemy soldiers and explosives. Once the area is clear, your squad dismounts automatically and advances toward the river.

REGROUP AT THE SMOKE

The river crossing is now secure. All that remains is to regroup with your squad at the red smoke on the opposite side of the river. Wade across the river, then head up the road to the smoke to complete this objective and get new orders.

Cross the river to get to the red smoke.

CLEAR THE HILLTOP FARM OF ANY HOSTILE FORCES.

- PROCEED TOWARD THE WEST FARM
- PICK UP THE ROCKET LAUNCHER
- ELIMINATE ALL ENEMIES
- DESTROY THE LIGHT TANK
- REGROUP AT THE SMOKE
- REGROUP AT THE SMOKE

Collectibles in this area: 1
Gold in this area: 0

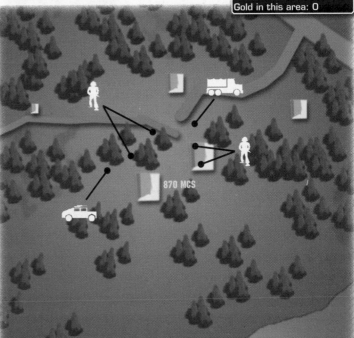

Ammo and a vehicle—what more could a soldier want?

Your new orders are to clear a farm located to the northeast of your position. It is a good distance away, so take the nearby enemy vehicle. If needed, stop by the ammo box and reload so you are ready for the next fight. Once your squad is aboard, drive down the road toward your objective.

PROCEED TOWARD THE WEST FARM

Turn off the road here.

Clear out all enemy soldiers from this house.

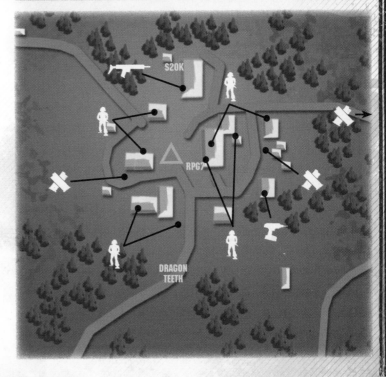

Follow the road until it makes a sharp left turn. Instead of continuing down the road, turn right onto a path and follow it to a house where a couple of enemy vehicles are parked. There are a few enemy soldiers here, so stay in the vehicle and switch seats to man the machine gun. Try to eliminate as many enemies as possible before disembarking. If there are still soldiers inside, launch a grenade to blow a hole in the building and then move in to clear it out. Inside you can find an 870 MCS shotgun. Pick it up to unlock another collectible, then pick up your XM8 again since it will be more useful than a shotgun for the remainder of this mission.

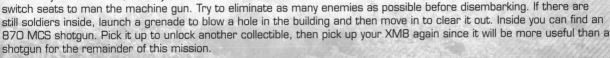

PRIMA Official Game Guide

BATTLEFIELD BAD COMPANY

Welcome · Basic Training · Infantry · Vehicles · Campaign · Multiplayer · Appendix

Welcome to Bad Company | Acta non Verba | Crossing Over | Par for the Course | Air Force One | Crash and Grab | Ghost Town

Take this road to the right.

If your vehicle took any damage, repair it with the power tool, then load back up and drive to the main road. Turn left at the main road and drive toward the farm. However, at the next intersection, turn to the right and follow another road around to approach the farm from the east. If you continue north to approach the farm from the south, you will run into anti-vehicle obstacles. As you near the farm, get ready for some action.

ELIMINATE ALL ENEMIES

Enemy soldiers near the house by the road and on top of the grain silo fire at your vehicle as you enter the farm. Be sure the enemies near the edge of the farm have been dealt with before continuing on or

Drive into the farm, letting your squad man the machine gun.

they will be able to fire at you from behind while other enemies attack from the front.

The machine gun in the northern building is a major threat. Kill the gunner and use it to clear out the enemies.

Once you enter the farm, stop and disembark just short of the tall building in the northern part of this area. A machine gun is positioned in the loft and would make short work of your vehicle. Blow a hole through the eastern wall and rush into this building. Kill any enemies on the ground floor, then climb up the ladder to the loft to take out the gunner. You can now man the machine gun and use it to eliminate enemies around the farm.

The loft is an awesome sniper perch.

After killing as many enemies as you can with the machine gun, switch back to your assault rifle. You may need to shoot areas the machine gun can't fire at or launch grenades at buildings to expose soldiers hiding inside. The minimap shows you where the remaining enemies are located.

If you decide to assault the farm from a different direction or on foot, you will need to deal with the machine gun in the northern building as quickly as possible. Since it is behind sandbags, launch grenades at this

Use the grenade launcher to take out the machine gunner in the northern building.

threat to destroy it before clearing your way through the rest of the buildings. There are ammo boxes to the east and west if you need more bullets or grenades.

REGROUP AT THE SMOKE

After all enemies in the farm have been neutralized, make your way to the red smoke which is placed near the northern building. Once you get there, be ready for some quick action.

The farm is clear.

PICK UP THE ROCKET LAUNCHER

An IFV busts out of the garage door of the northern building.

The RPG is in the central barn.

As soon as you meet up with your squad, you hear a growling sound. An enemy armored vehicle bursts out of the northern building and fires at you. Grenades and machine gun fire will not stop this type of vehicle. You need an RPG. Even though Haggard carries one, get an RPG of your own. Sprint into the central barn to find an RPG on some weapons cases in the south-western corner. Pick it up.

DESTROY THE LIGHT TANK

Stay low inside the barn and use its walls for cover. The minimap shows you the location of the enemy vehicle. Maneuver around so you can take a quick shot at the tank—preferably from the rear or side—and then

Use the RPG to destroy the armored vehicle.

quickly duck back behind cover while you load another rocket. It usually takes a couple hits to destroy this vehicle. Don't forget to heal yourself if you take damage. The weapons on the vehicle can cause a lot of damage in a short amount of time, so don't let yourself be killed.

REGROUP AT THE SMOKE

Back to the squad.

Now that the new threat has been dealt with, another red smoke grenade has been placed to prepare for a pick up from a friendly helicopter—this time in the southern part of the farm. Meet up with the squad to wait for your ride.

NOTE ★★

If you have not picked up a S20K shotgun to unlock this collectible yet, there is one in the northern building on the ground floor.

★ OBJECTIVE IMPALA ★

CLEAR OUT THE ENEMY ANTI-AIRCRAFT GUNS IN THE AREA TO ALLOW ALLIED AIRPOWER TO OPERATE UNMOLESTED.

▶ PROCEED TOWARD THE ANTI-AIRCRAFT BASE   ▶ PICK UP C4 EXPLOSIVES   ▶ DESTROY THE ANTI-AIRCRAFT GUNS   ▶ REGROUP AT THE SMOKE

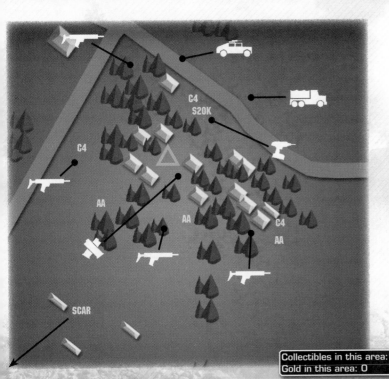

Here is a ride to get to the next objective.

A helo was sent to pick up your squad. However, the enemy shot it down before it could get to you. Your new objective is to take out those AA guns before they shoot down more friendly aircraft. Climb aboard one of the armored jeeps at the farm after topping off your ammo at one of the ammo boxes. Drive east out of the farm and follow the road to the south.

Collectibles in this area: 1
Gold in this area: 0

PRIMA Official Game Guide

Welcome • Basic Training • Infantry • Vehicles • Campaign • Multiplayer • Appendix

Welcome to Bad Company | Acta non Verba | Crossing Over | Par for the Course | Air Force One | Crash and Grab | Ghost Town

The house on the left has a collectible waiting for you.

When you come to the intersection, rather than turning left toward the objective, drive straight ahead and through the wooden fence and across the field until you come to another road. Turn left and head east until you come to some buildings near the damaged bridge. The house in the western corner of the intersection contains a SCAR. Pick it up to unlock the collectible, then pick up your XM8. Return to the vehicle and drive northeast from the intersection.

PROCEED TOWARD THE ANTI-AIRCRAFT BASE

Man the vehicle's machine gun and clear out this AA position.

Once you are nearly due south of the eastern AA gun, turn into the field on your left and drive north. As you approach, your squad mate on the machine gun engages enemies in the area, including the soldier manning the machine gun. Since you are coming from the south, this machine gun, which is positioned pointing west, can't hit you. Switch seats and man the vehicle's machine gun to take out any soldiers who come toward you.

PICK UP C4 EXPLOSIVES

Clear out the machine gun position in the north, then pick up some C4.

Don't get out of the vehicle yet. Switch back to the driver's seat and head north to the road. Turn left and follow the road to some sandbags with weapons cases. Let your squad clear out any nearby enemies before disembarking. A machine gun position is located to the west. The gun can't turn to hit you, but the gunner can use his personal weapon. Kill him, then head back to the sandbags to pick up some C4. You have to leave your RPG there, but don't worry—you'll come back for it.

DESTROY THE ANTI-AIRCRAFT GUNS

Clear out soldiers as you advance to the AA guns.

From the sandbags, head southwest along a path. Stay crouched down and move cautiously as you head to the AA guns. There are still some enemies around. By using this path, you will avoid the other two machine gun positions which are still manned.

After you have cleared out the anti-aircraft base, place a C4 charge on each of the AA guns. You can place multiple charges by pressing the reload button to switch from the detonator to another charge. Once you have all three guns ready to blow, use the detonator to destroy all of the AA guns at the same time.

Place a C4 charge on each AA gun.

Blow all three charges at the same time.

REGROUP AT THE SMOKE

Now head back to the sandbags where you left the RPG. Before picking it up, get a power tool and repair your vehicle if necessary. Then get your RPG and move to the red smoke to complete this objective.

Back to the red smoke.

You can also go after the anti–aircraft base before you pick up the SCAR. You will have to deal with the western machine gun positions as you approach along the road from the farm. The best tactic is to drive fast to the sandbags where the C4 is located, and then deal with the machine gun positions from outside their firing arcs. Another strategy for this objective is to get the SCAR and clear out the eastern AA gun. C4 can be found at this position. Then begin clearing out the base from this location first. While picking up the C4 is an objective, you don't have to use it to destroy the AA guns. The RPG does the job as well.

OBJECTIVE BRONCO

INVESTIGATE AND SECURE THE EAST FARM.

- PROCEED TO THE EAST FARM
- ELIMINATE ALL ENEMIES
- ELIMINATE INCOMING REINFORCEMENTS
- REGROUP AT THE SMOKE
- FOLLOW THE CONVOY
- REGROUP AT THE SMOKE

Collectibles in this area: 0
Gold in this area: 0

You can also drive north from the anti–aircraft base and approach the east farm from the south. However, by travelling that direction, you run into soldiers out in the fields and come under fire from a machine gun in the loft of the barn as soon as you get close to the farm.

ELIMINATE ALL ENEMIES

Man the machine gun and clear out enemies like the one on the grain silo.

PROCEED TO THE EAST FARM

Your orders are to secure another farm. This one is to the north of your position. Climb into an armored jeep and drive to the east, following the road as it turns to the

Drive to the east farm.

north and then eventually back around to the west. Along the way, in a little shack on the side of the road, you can pick up an XM8. However, you should already have one that you picked up earlier.

As you enter the farm, stay along the left side of the road. A machine gun is positioned on the second floor of the barn in the western part of the farm. Since it can damage your vehicle, keep a building between the machine gun and your vehicle. Switch seats to man your machine gun and clear out as many soldiers as possible. Also use this weapon to shoot down the wooden fences in front of the houses, which might be hiding enemies.

Head around the southern side of the farm and shoot at the explosive crates to destroy the enemy machine gun.

PRiMA Official Game Guide

BAD COMPANY BATTLEFIELD

Welcome · Basic Training · Infantry · Vehicles · Campaign · Multiplayer · Appendix

Welcome to Bad Company | Acta non Verba | Crossing Over | Par for the Course | Air Force One | Crash and Grab | Ghost Town

Not all enemies in the farm can be killed from inside the vehicle. Dismount and make your way west along the south side of the farm. Your goal is the main threat in the area—the machine gun in the barn. Use the house for cover as you approach, killing soldiers who come at you along the way. When you get the machine gun in your sights, don't launch a grenade. Instead, aim for the explosive crates near the machine gun and shoot them. The resulting explosion takes out the machine gun and the soldier as well. Now finish off any remaining soldiers in the farm. Be sure to stop by the ammo box by the road intersection to stock up for the next part of this objective.

TIP

If you need an RPG, you can find a couple on the second floors of the two-story houses along the road.

ELIMINATE INCOMING REINFORCEMENTS

Blow out the northern part of the barn's roof so you can shoot at the enemy armored jeep that arrives from the north.

The barn loft is a great position for shooting at enemy reinforcements.

Once you have initially secured the farm, more soldiers arrive from across the bridge to the north. Get to the barn and climb up the stairs. Launch a grenade at a northern section of the roof near the front of the barn to create a hole through which you can shoot. Then shoot an enemy armored jeep with the RPG. Switch back to your assault rifle and kill the soldiers that arrive from the north as well. Stay crouched and use the cover of the walls to help protect you from enemy fire.

Fire two rockets at the IFV to destroy it as quickly as possible.

After fighting off the first reinforcements, more arrive from the east. The main threat from this direction is an IFV. Take it out with the RPG as well. Fire a rocket and take cover while reloading. Repeat the process until the enemy vehicle is destroyed. Then finish off any remaining enemies to completely clear out the farm so the convoy can approach.

REGROUP AT THE SMOKE

Get back together with your squad.

Another enemy-held area has been cleared by Bad Company. Heal your wounds, stock up on ammo, and head to the red smoke to assemble with the other three members of your squad to await your next orders.

FOLLOW THE CONVOY

Hop in a nearby vehicle and follow the convoy.

Incoming fire!

Since you cleared out this farm, the convoy rolls through unmolested and continues across the bridge. Climb into one of the armored jeeps and take off after the convoy in case they need your help later on. As you drive down the road, the convoy comes under artillery fire. Get ready for another objective.

REGROUP AT THE SMOKE

Assemble near the water.

Quickly dismount from the vehicle before it is destroyed by the artillery fire and you are killed. Move to the left side of the road and continue to the red smoke to meet up with your squad and await new orders.

DESTROY THE RADAR JAMMERS ▸ REGROUP AT THE SMOKE ▸ MOVE IN AND SECURE THE BASE

Collectibles in this area: 0
Gold in this area: 0

The enemy artillery is on the other side of the water.

Command gives you some new orders. The artillery that bombarded the convoy is east of your current position. The Air Force wants to take it out. However, the enemy is jamming their radars, preventing the flyboys from getting a lock for their weapons. Your job is to move in and destroy the two radar jammers so airstrikes are able to smoke the artillery.

DESTROY THE RADAR JAMMERS

Move along the road as you head east.

Shoot soldiers as you make your way around the lake.

The radar jammers are located across a small lake. While you can try crossing the lake, since it is deep, you would have to swim and not be able to use your weapon. The better tactic is to go back to the road and follow it around the side of the lake. There are a couple of enemies on the far bank of the lake. Stay crouched while near the road and shoot both of them as soon as you get them into your sights.

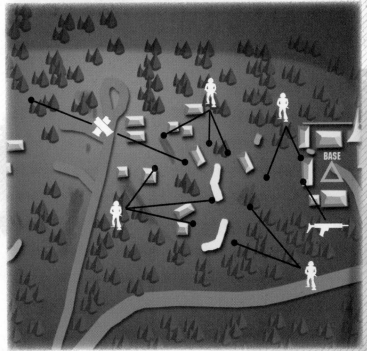

PRIMA Official Game Guide

BATTLEFIELD BAD COMPANY

Welcome • Basic Training • Infantry • Vehicles • Campaign • Multiplayer • Appendix

Welcome to Bad Company | Acta non Verba | Crossing Over | Par for the Course | Air Force One | Crash and Grab | Ghost Town

Use the RPG to take out the machine gun towers.

As you get around the lake, continue east by moving through a series of trenches. Stay to the south as much as possible and you should not run into any more soldiers as you advance toward the radar jammers. Up ahead are some towers. There is a total of three, but you can usually only see one or two until you get closer. Each of these towers contains a machine gun manned by an enemy soldier. They can make your life difficult, so take them out as soon as you see them. Use the RPG to destroy the wooden top half of these towers. Even if you don't destroy the machine gun, you usually kill the gunner with a single rocket. By the time you get near the southernmost tower, you should have been able to take out all three towers.

If you continue to stay to the south, you eventually follow a path that leads to the southern tower. Crouch down and use the nearby sandbags for cover as you engage the soldiers in this area. They usually

Clear out enemies near the jammers while using sandbags for cover.

come at you from the north and your squad helps you deal with them. Watch your minimap for enemy blips and clear out all the enemies you can before advancing farther into this area.

C4 can be found in the southern and middle towers.

Place two C4 charges on each radar jammer, then detonate.

Move into concrete lower level of the southern tower and pick up some C4. You have to drop your RPG for now, but be sure to pick it back up later. Place two charges on one of the radar jammers since one will not do the trick. You can either place both at one time and detonate, or

detonate each in turn. Repeat the process for the second radar jammer to complete this objective.

Instead of using the C4, you can also destroy the radar jammers with the RPG. It takes two rocket hits to destroy each jammer. If you need more ammo for the RPG, visit the ammo box in the northern tower.

REGROUP AT THE SMOKE

Before heading to the red smoke, pick up the RPG from where you left it and resupply at the ammo box in the northern tower. You need a full load out of ammo for the next task. Once you meet up with your squad at the smoke, you will be treated to a display of aerial firepower.

The Air Force flies in and neutralizes all of the enemy artillery.

MOVE IN AND SECURE THE BASE

Use the machine gun to take out some enemies.

You have one more objective for this mission—clear out the enemy base to the east. Use the machine gun near where your squad regrouped to kill nearby enemies. While you can't get them all, you can at least get a couple. As your squad moves toward the base, leave the machine gun and take the southern route through the trenches toward the base.

The grenade launcher works well for taking down the enemies along the way.

Keep an eye on the minimap so these enemies don't surprise you as they pop out from behind a rock.

The squad assembles at the enemy base.

Stay crouched down and move cautiously as you make your way toward the base. There are lots of soldiers waiting to ambush you. The minimap is your best friend since it usually shows you where the enemies are located before you can see them. Stay on your toes because the enemies come after you, and hide behind cover as they take shots at you. If you take damage, duck behind cover of your own and use the auto injector for some quick healing.

Why are there mercenaries at this Russian base?

As you get closer to the base, the enemies look different. You are no longer fighting Russians in standard uniforms, but mercenaries dressed in black with newer weapons. They are a bit tougher to kill. However, a shot to the head will still do the trick.

These aren't Russians, they're mercenaries!

Sweetwater remembers that these mercenaries are usually paid in gold—and it looks like this one was carrying his paycheck.

TIP

You quickly expend your rifle ammo during this part of the mission. Either pick up ammo from dead enemies by walking over their assault rifles or stop by the ammo box in the central area of the map.

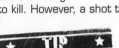

In Bad Company, moral questions are not much of a problem. There is probably more gold around, just waiting for you to find.

Don't rush up the path leading to the base. It is defended by a machine gun. While you can shoot the gunner, it is usually better to eliminate this threat from a distance. The grenade launcher is always an option, but if you don't hit the gunner with your first grenade, he may shoot at you. Instead, blow away the threat with a long-range RPG shot. A mercenary waits in front of the base at the bottom of the trail to ambush you. Kill him, then head into the base to complete the mission.

A machine gun position defends the enemy base.

PRIMA Official Game Guide

BATTLEFIELD BAD COMPANY

Welcome · Basic Training · Infantry · Vehicles · Campaign · Multiplayer · Appendix

Welcome to Bad Company I **Acta non Verba** I Crossing Over I Par for the Course I Air Force One I Crash and Grab I Ghost Town

ACTA NON VERBA

Collectibles in this mission: 1
Gold in this mission: 5

With Uncle Sam busy with the war, and the gold bar so small, we thought we would split it four ways. Not that everybody was happy with that arrangement, however. Now we head to Zabograd, an important harbor twenty clicks behind enemy lines. The Army is launching an offensive and we are the first ones to go in.

★ PROCEED TOWARDS THE RIVER BANK ★

MOVE DOWN TO THE RIVER BANK AND WAIT FOR FURTHER ORDERS.

▸ SEARCH THE HOUSE   ▸ MOVE OUT   ▸ ELIMINATE ALL ENEMIES   ▸ REGROUP AT THE SMOKE

A new mission begins.

The chopper drops your squad off near an abandoned house a distance from Zabograd to avoid alerting the enemy. Haggard notices a sign in front of the house. The Latin motto is the same one you found on the dead mercenary. It seems like the Russians aren't the only ones you will be dealing with.

Collectibles in this area: 0
Gold in this area: 2

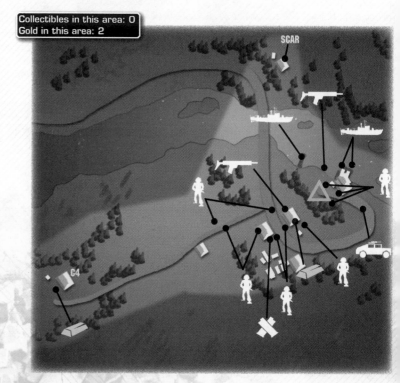

SEARCH THE HOUSE

Break open the door with your knife.

You want to find cases like these during missions. They contain gold.

Your first task is to search the abandoned house. Since it might be booby trapped, your squad chose you—the new guy—to search it. Walk up to the door and break it down by pressing the knife button. Don't worry, there are no traps and no enemies in the house. However, there is some C4 on a stack of weapons cases. Pick the C4 up—it comes in handy later. Also in the room you see another case with the mercenary logo on it. Open it to find a gold bar. Maybe your squad won't have to share that first gold bar after all.

MOVE OUT

Now that you have secured the house—and the gold—it is time to move on. Exit the house and start marching down the road. Since you are exposed along the road and there are enemies up ahead, walk in the

The road leads to your next objectives.

grass and through the trees along the right side of the road.

ELIMINATE ALL ENEMIES

Take down these two soldiers patrolling the road as they walk away from you.

As you advance, your squad members let you know they see enemies up ahead. Crouch down and keep moving through cover adjacent to the road. A couple soldiers are patrolling along the road near a shed. Bring up your ironsights and wait for the soldiers to turn around and walk away from you. Aim for the farthest soldier first and drop him with a burst of rifle fire. Then kill the second soldier to clear the roadway.

Clear the small house from a distance.

Advance through a field toward the small house. The two-story house behind the small house has a machine gun on the second floor, so use the small house as cover by keeping it between you and the machine gun.

A soldier is inside the small house, so watch the windows and neutralize him before you get to the small house.

Move up next to the small house, but don't walk through the doorway yet. The soldier manning the machine gun has a field of fire to the doorway through a window on the other side of the small house. However,

Shoot through the window of the small house to kill the machine gunner.

you also have the same field of fire back at the machine gunner. Crouch down next to the doorway and then strafe to the side to look through the doorway and window. Shoot the gunner before he can hurt you or your squad.

TIP

Notice the ammo box behind the small house. That means you can go hog wild with not only your rifle, but also your grenade launcher. Try taking out the machine gun by lobbing grenades over the top of the small house. Also use grenades to blow holes in the sides of the buildings. An enemy is hiding beneath a window and taking pot shots at you. Aim at the wall below the window to take out the wall and soldier in one shot!

Another case is upstairs.

Enter the small house and use it for cover as you clear out other soldiers coming from the direction of the larger house. Your squad helps you eliminate them. Now clear out the large house. Use

grenades and rifle fire to do the job, then stop by the ammo box by the small house to restock. The large house has a mercenary sign outside, so check it out. Climb up the stairs to find another mercenary case. Open it to pick up another gold bar.

PRIMA Official Game Guide

BAD COMPANY
BATTLEFIELD

Welcome · Basic Training · Infantry · Vehicles · Campaign · Multiplayer · Appendix

Welcome to Bad Company | **Acta non Verba** | Crossing Over | Par for the Course | Air Force One | Crash and Grab | Ghost Town

The second floor is a great location for sniping down on enemies near the dock.

While upstairs, move to the window on the eastern side of the house. From this spot, shoot down on the three soldiers by the docks. Check the minimap to see their locations. If you fire at them, they usually come toward you. If not, launch some grenades to destroy their cover or—even better—them.

of the river. Cross by the destroyed bridge if you want this weapon. However, your M416 works best for the next part of this mission.

Another red smoke rendezvous.

Whether or not you decide to get the SCAR, hoof it to the red smoke to meet up with your squad and receive new orders.

REGROUP AT THE SMOKE

Now that all enemies have been eliminated in this area, you need to move down to the dock area to the smoke. Before you do that, you can pick up a silenced SCAR from a house on the northern side

Head across this destroyed bridge to the north if you want to pick up a SCAR.

OPERATION BACKFIELD

REACH AND DESTROY WEAPONS AND FUEL TO CRIPPLE ENEMY SUPPLY LINES.

▸ **DESTROY THE MISSILE LAUNCHERS**　▸ **DESTROY THE FUEL STORAGE**　▸ **REGROUP AT THE SMOKE**

You have your choice of two different modes of transportation.

Two new objectives have been assigned to your squad. Before you go after the missile launchers, there is a mercenary base along the river you can clear out. At the dock, take either a patrol boat or an armored jeep. The boat is a better choice with two automatic grenade launchers compared to the jeep's single machine gun. As you head east along the river, engage two enemy patrol boats. Your squad can deal with them while you drive, or switch to a gunner's seat to sink the boats yourself. Continue on to the base located to the south of and across the river from the missile launchers. Several soldiers defend the base.

Clear out the soldiers at the base.

Drive the patrol boat right up onto the docks or bank near the base. Use the grenade launcher to eliminate as many enemies as possible before disembarking. Then fire your rifle to finish off any remaining enemies. Some will try to hide in the building or behind stone walls. Remember to check your minimap to see where they are located.

That case in the excavation looks familiar. Open it to find more gold.

Once you have cleared the enemies out the base, notice another mercenary sign near an excavation area. Walk down into the excavation area to find a case which contains another gold bar. Take the gold and head back to the docks. Jump into a new boat and move to the objective.

C4

MISSILE
LAUNCHERS

M416

870 MCS

C4

FUEL
TANKS

870 MCS

PRIMA Official Game Guide

★ TIP ★

In the mercenary base, you can also pick up an 870 MCS
shotgun. While it is great for close-quarters fighting, you will
need the range of your M416 as well as its grenade launcher
for dealing with enemies.

DESTROY THE MISSILE LAUNCHERS

*Drive the patrol boat to this dock and use the grenade
launcher to bombard the building where the missile
launchers are located.*

BATTLEFIELD BAD COMPANY

Welcome · Basic Training · Infantry · Vehicles · Campaign · Multiplayer · Appendix

Welcome to Bad Company | **Acta non Verba** | Crossing Over | Par for the Course | Air Force One | Crash and Grab | Ghost Town

No matter which vehicle you used before, you need a patrol boat to get across the river. Drive it to a dock south of the objective building and then switch seats to fire the front grenade launcher at enemies near the building. While you won't be able to see many soldiers, just fire around the building to knock down as many walls as possible and hopefully clear out those soldiers patrolling around the southern part of the building.

Approach the building, clearing enemies as you go. Stop by the ammo box to restock before you enter through the nearby doorway. There is usually at least one soldier right inside the building. Unfor-

There are enemies all over the building—on the ground floor, second floor, and even the roof.

tunately, the walls of this building are very thick, so you can't blow a hole to enter where you want. Watch out for enemies on the second floor catwalks who like to fire down on you.

Use C4 to blow up the missile launchers.

Once you clear the first and second floors, place a C4 charge on each of the three missile launchers. Exit the building and blow the C4 to complete one of your objectives. However, the fun is not over. Enemy reinforcements arrive from both the north and south. The northern counterattack includes an armored jeep. Since you can use this vehicle later, don't destroy it. Instead, take careful aim at the gunner and kill him to neutralize the jeep as a threat. Then focus on eliminating the rest of the enemies in the area.

Don't destroy the armored jeep.

NOTE ★★

If you do not have the C4 from the house at the start of the mission, find some on the first floor in the northern part of the building. An M416 is on the rooftop if you need one.

DESTROY THE FUEL STORAGE

Drive north under the bridge, then across the bridge to get to the fuel storage area.

The fuel storage area is across the river to the east. Since you spared the armored jeep, jump in and get moving. There are two ways to get to the next objective. You can head straight across the river, but this puts you in the sights of a machine gun position. Your other option is to cross the river by driving on the bridge. To get up to the bridge, drive north under the bridge and follow the dirt road around to the left to get to the roadway of the bridge. Then drive east across the river and avoid the machine gun fire.

If you drive across the river, you have to deal with a machine gun that can damage your vehicle.

Continue across the bridge to the other side. As you approach the next area, soldiers shoot at you from the windows of the barracks. You can either let your squad deal with them while you drive, or switch seats and gun them down

Stop on the bridge just north of the machine gun position, get out, and fire at the explosive barrels to destroy this threat.

yourself. Turn into the entrance to this base and stop. Man the machine gun and kill as many enemies as you can in the large building as well as in the barracks. Watch the damage meter on your vehicle. If it gets close to being destroyed, get out before you are killed.

Use the vehicle machine gun to help clear out this base.

Move through the barracks to clear them of any enemies who might be hiding.

tanks on the first floor. You only need one charge per set of tanks. When one goes, the nearby tanks will as well. Exit the building, select the detonator, and pull the trigger to watch the explosions rock the building.

Plant the charges and then detonate them for some major fireworks.

An 870 MCS shotgun is in one of the barracks. Pick it up and clear out the large building with it since most combat will be up close. Be sure to get your M416 before leaving this area. You can also find C4 on the second floor of the fuel building.

Dismount from the vehicle and work your way through the barracks to make sure all enemies in this area have been eliminated. You don't want these soldiers sneaking up behind you while you are clearing out the large building. Next, head into the large building and terminate all the enemies inside. A good place to start is in the south. Climb up the stairway and clear out the second level. From here you can fire down on any enemies who haven't been killed already by your squad. Place a charge on the fuel tanks in the north and south on the second floor as well as another charge on the large

REGROUP AT THE SMOKE

Having completed another objective, it is time to regroup with your squad. Before you move to the smoke, restock your ammo at the ammo box and pick up your M416 if you swapped it for another weapon.

You just blew up the enemy's weapons and fuel. What are you going to do now? Go to the red smoke!

SECURE THE BRIDGE

USE THE MORTAR STRIKE TO ELIMINATE THE SOLDIERS ON THE BRIDGE.

▶ PICK UP MORTAR STRIKE ▶ ELIMINATE THE SOLDIERS ON THE BRIDGE ▶ REGROUP AT THE SMOKE

PICK UP MORTAR STRIKE

Enemy units have moved onto the bridge over the river. There are infantry as well as two armored jeeps. Friendly fire support is not available. However, Sweetwater identifies a Russian mortar

This little device can bring down a lot of firepower on the targets of your choice.

designator on a weapons case in the same room as your squad. Pick it up.

ELIMINATE THE SOLDIERS ON THE BRIDGE

Aim at one of the enemy vehicles and hold down the fire trigger. Within a few seconds, a Russian mortar battery will send a fire mission to your designated coordinates.

While you may be tempted to head back to the main road leading to the bridge, you would expose yourself to enemy fire. Instead, exit this base through the south entrance and move around the corner to the west. Stay crouched and continue moving until you see the enemy vehicles on the bridge. Switch to the mortar strike and aim at one of the vehicles. Hold down the fire button to send the coordinates and then watch the mortar rounds hit. Not only can they destroy the vehicles and infantry, this bombardment also takes out sections of the bridge. Wait for the device to recharge, and then target and knock out the second vehicle.

Welcome · Basic Training · Infantry · Vehicles · Campaign · Multiplayer · Appendix

Welcome to Bad Company | **Acta non Verba** | Crossing Over | Par for the Course | Air Force One | Crash and Grab | Ghost Town

★ OBJECTIVE OFFSIDE ★

DESTROY THE ANTI-VEHICLE WEAPONS TO SECURE A PATH FOR THE U.S. FORCES.

▭▷ REGROUP AT THE SMOKE   ▭▷ DESTROY THE STATIONARY GUNS   ▭▷ REGROUP AT THE SMOKE

Collectibles in this area: 0
Gold in this area: 1

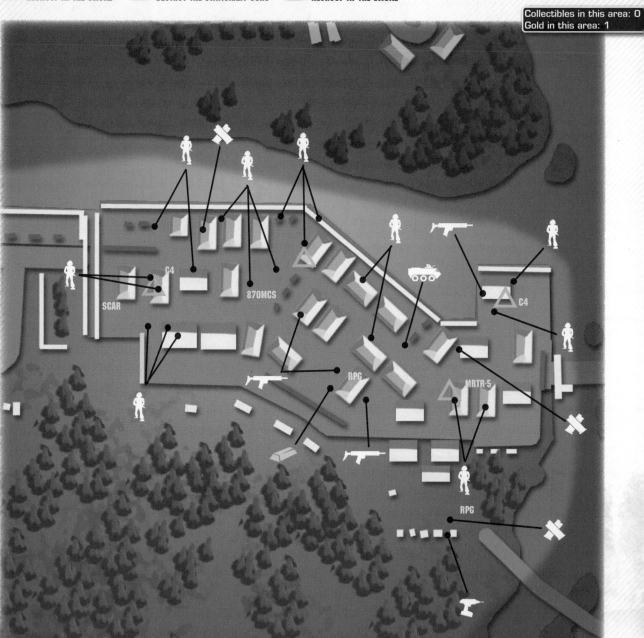

Drive back across the river to get onto the main road.

Your new orders are to move to a designated location on the other side of the river. Since you just blew out sections of the bridge, you must cross the river at the ford. Find an armored jeep to the west of the fuel base. Get your squad in and then follow the dirt road across the river to the weapon base where you blew up the missile launchers. Drive down the dirt road which leads to the north and then winds around to the main road.

REGROUP AT THE SMOKE

Watch out for an enemy armored jeep. Shoot and destroy it with your machine gun.

Follow the main road to the northwest and around a series of turns. Along the way, enemy soldiers in an armored jeep of their own attack. Switch to the gunner's seat and use the machine gun to destroy the enemy vehicle before it causes too much damage to your own vehicle. Finish off the dismounted soldiers, then drive on.

Continue down the road until you come to some ruins near a left-hand turn. Some enemy soldiers block your path to the red smoke. Kill as many as possible with your machine gun before disembarking from the vehicle.

Stop by these ruins and engage the enemies.

Clear out any remaining enemies in the area. Use the minimap to help locate them. Once the ruins have been secured, continue to the red smoke to regroup with your squad and receive further orders.

The red smoke is calling to you.

DESTROY THE STATIONARY GUNS

Time to take it downtown.

The U.S. armored column met heavy resistance as it tried to enter the city. The enemy has set up four stationary guns. Until they are eliminated, the Army will not risk sending tanks through. Your squad has been assigned to go into the city and destroy those guns.

Use the mortar strike designator to call in some artillery fire onto buildings in the city before you even enter.

In addition to the stationary guns, which are essentially guided anti-tank missile launchers, you also face machine gun positions and lots of soldiers. There is no time limit, so take it easy and be cautious. A good tactic is to use the mortar strike designator to call down fire on buildings in which you suspect enemies are hiding. This can destroy some of the stationary and machine guns, or at least blow away the walls of buildings to reveal the enemies inside.

Watch for soldiers moving throughout the city. Some will come after you rather than wait to ambush your squad.

The first gun is located just east of the entrance to the city.

As you enter the city, be ready to fight. The first gun is near the entrance and will fire once the gunner sees you. These missiles can really hurt you, so take cover and then shoot the gunner with your rifle.

You can also call in a mortar strike on the building to try and eliminate the gunner and gun all at once.

Enter the building with the first gun and pick up some C4. Place a charge on the side of the gun, then detonate it to get rid of one of the four guns.

Keep an eye on your minimap as you make your way to the east along the northern street to check for hidden enemies. Be ready to shoot at soldiers that jump out from doors or fire from upstairs windows. When this occurs, quickly take cover and then return fire. If they are hiding, blow a hole in a wall with your grenade launcher.

Advance along the northern street, clearing out soldiers as you go.

PRIMA Official Game Guide

BATTLEFIELD BAD COMPANY

Welcome · Basic Training · Infantry · Vehicles · Campaign · Multiplayer · Appendix

Welcome to Bad Company | Acta non Verba | Crossing Over | Par for the Course | Air Force One | Crash and Grab | Ghost Town

Don't be afraid to use the mortar strike a lot. While you don't need to destroy every building in the city, those containing machine guns or soldiers are good targets.

A mortar strike on a building will usually eliminate most of the building's cover.

As you approach the next stationary gun, an IFV appears down the road to the east. It will not come after you, but its weapons are deadly. If you still have the mortar strike designator, call in a strike on

Call in a mortar strike against the enemy IFV.

the vehicle. One or two strikes should do the job. However, it can be dangerous standing out in the open to target the vehicle for the strike. As long as you stay out of this street, the IFV can't really hurt you. Therefore, you can engage it later on and advance along the river on the north side of town, or along the southern street.

The northeastern gun is in this house overlooking the water.

You can use this gun to destroy the IFV. Just be sure to take out a section of wall so you have a clear line of fire.

Advance along the river on the northern side of town to avoid the IFV and enemy fire from the center of town. The building overlooking the river on the eastern side of town contains one of the stationary guns as well as a machine gun. Either destroy the building with a mortar strike or shoot the gunners with your assault rifle from long range. Then use the gun to shoot and destroy the IFV. Two missile hits will smoke that vehicle. There is also some C4 in this building you can then use to destroy the gun.

You can also advance down the southern street to avoid the IFV. Continue to the mercenary headquarters and clear it out. This building is defended by two machine guns as well as soldiers. Once it is clear, you can pick up an RPG inside which you can use against the IFV. Also, don't forget to grab a gold bar while you are at it.

While advancing along the southern road, look for this mercenary sign. It shows that this is a mercenary headquarters. Not only can you find an RPG inside, but also another gold bar.

Silence those machine guns.

Shoot the gunners manning the machine guns from the side so they can't turn their guns to fire at you. It is important to clear out the machine guns since they can really hurt your squad if not silenced as quickly as possible. As you systematically advance through the city, clearing as you go, destroy the stationary guns to complete the objective.

REGROUP AT THE SMOKE

Head out this gate and meet up with your squad.

After destroying all four guns, not just the killing the gunners, you will be ordered to move to the red smoke south of the eastern part of town. Be sure to pick up the gold bar in the mercenary headquarters before exiting this part of the city.

▱▱▱▶ KEEP THE TANKS ALIVE   ▱▱▱▶ REGROUP AT THE SMOKE

Restock on ammo and pick up the power tool.

Soon after regrouping, the U.S. tanks arrive. Your new job is to make sure they get to the other side of Zabograd. Since you are their support, take along the power tool to repair any damage they take along the way.

KEEP THE TANKS ALIVE

Climb into the lead tank and man the machine gun.

Collectibles in this area: 1
Gold in this area: 1

Move up to the lead tank and climb in. While you can't drive the tank, you can man the machine gun and attack enemies along the way. The first threats appear near a house on the right side of your route. Use

The gun view provides a reticle and makes it easier to engage enemies.

the machine gun to mow down soldiers armed with RPGs. Then dismount and climb up the hill to the house. Clear out any remaining soldiers inside, then move in to pick up a M249 light machine gun which is a collectible.

This house contains a light machine gun. Go pick it up.

Exit the house and head back down to the tanks. You can continue to cover them using your M249, focusing on enemies with RPGs first. You can also climb back into the

lead tank to man its machine gun. Keep track of how much damage the tanks are taking. The lead and second tank are the ones to worry about the most. When they start taking damage, dismount and use the power tool to repair them. You will usually have to make repairs while the tanks are rolling.

Shoot soldiers attacking the tanks.

Keep those tanks repaired.

Near the ammo box, an IFV will appear and start firing on your tanks. You can pick up an RPG by the ammo box to attack the enemy vehicle. However, it is usually better to let your tanks take care of the enemy with their main guns while you repair any damage the tanks may incur. More soldiers will continue to attack from the sides of the path all the way to the park outside of the city. It is usually best to stay in the tank and deal with them.

PRIMA Official Game Guide

BAD COMPANY
BATTLEFIELD

Welcome · Basic Training · Infantry · Vehicles · Campaign · Multiplayer · Appendix

Welcome to Bad Company | **Acta non Verba** | Crossing Over | Par for the Course | Air Force One | Crash and Grab | Ghost Town

Ride the tank all the way to the end.

REGROUP AT THE SMOKE

Dismount from the tank once you have escorted the column safely to the entrance of the city. Before you move to the red smoke, walk to the south-western corner of the park area. Just outside the

Met your squad in the park.

park, there is a mercenary case. Open it to find the last bar of gold for this mission. Move to the red smoke and meet up with your squad to await your next orders.

★ ASSAULT EAST ZABOGRAD ★

INVESTIGATE THE COMMAND POST AND DESTROY THE COMMUNICATIONS EQUIPMENT.

▸ DESTROY THE RADIO EQUIPMENT   ▸ REGROUP AT THE SMOKE

Enter East Zabograd.

While the tanks are rolling into the city through a main gate, lead your squad in through the breach in the wall.

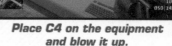

Place C4 on the equipment and blow it up.

Work your way through the city to the western part where the objective is located. The building is filled with soldiers, so throw or launch grenades into the building to clear it out before rushing in. Pick up some

C4 at the foot of the staircase and then head up the stairs. At the top, face east and be ready to shoot a soldier through the window. He is in the attic of a building across the street, protecting the radio equipment. Kill him, place the C4 on the equipment, and blow it up to complete the objective.

DESTROY THE RADIO EQUIPMENT

Fight through the streets and inside the buildings.

Zabrograd is filled with enemies. There are machine guns in several positions along the eastern half of the city with some stationary missile launchers in the western part of the city. All are on the second floor of houses, so look up as well as around and duck into houses for cover when you come under attack. Just be ready to fight inside the house in case an enemy is already hiding there.

A soldier is waiting to ambush you from a rooftop across the street from the radio equipment.

★ TIP ★

The stationary gun positions can be deadly if you are not paying attention to them. Unlike a machine gun, which makes a lot of noise, you may not detect these missile launchers until their missile hits near you. Luckily, the soldiers manning these weapons do not have a shield, so they can be easily killed with rifle fire.

C4

RPG

MRT

RPG

M416

REGROUP AT THE SMOKE

After the radio equipment is destroyed, head downstairs and meet up with your squad to await new orders. There is still some fighting left to do in Zabograd.

This smoke is near the destroyed radio equipment.

PRIMA Official Game Guide

Welcome · Basic Training · Infantry · Vehicles · Campaign · Multiplayer · Appendix

Welcome to Bad Company | **Acta non Verba** | Crossing Over | Par for the Course | Air Force One | Crash and Grab | Ghost Town

GROUNDHOG DOWN

PROTECT THE U.S. TANK UNTIL REINFORCEMENTS ARRIVE.

🔸 PROTECT THE U.S. TANK   🔸 REGROUP AT THE SMOKE

The tank you need to protect is in the central square by the fountain.

Head east to the middle of the town where you find the tank you must protect. Rush over to the fountain to restock at the ammo box and to pick up the RPG, which will come in handy.

Use the RPG to take out the enemy IFV.

More vehicles arrive. An IFV leads another armored jeep through the northern gate. Fire the RPG to eliminate the IFV first. It takes two hits to neutralize this threat. If you run out of rockets, pick up the RPG on the weapons case near the machine gun for more ammo. Then take out the armored jeep with the remainder of your rockets. Finally get back on the machine gun to finish off the infantry in the area.

PROTECT THE U.S. TANK

This machine gun is a great position from which to defend the tank.

The best position for defending the tank is the building directly behind it. Climb up the stairs to the second floor and man the machine gun. It has a shield that helps protect you from enemy small arms fire. Soldiers begin advancing on the tank from the north and east. Gun them down before they can get in too close. Those carrying RPGs should be your first priority. Watch for them to take up positions in the second floors of the buildings to the north of you. Eventually an armored jeep drives into the area. Either use your RPG to waste it or just shoot at it with the machine gun until it is destroyed.

REGROUP AT THE SMOKE

Red smoke time.

Meet up with the squad and get ready to leave Zabograd and go after the mercenaries.

SECURE HARBOR

REACH AND SECURE THE HARBOR BEFORE THE RUSSIANS EVACUATE.

🔸 REACH HARBOR   🔸 REACH TRUCKS

You now must head to the harbor to try to stop the Russians from evacuating. Before you leave, pick up the mortar strike located near the tank you just protected.

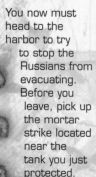

Climb into the humvee to get to your next objective.

With it in hand, advance to the humvee to the north and climb in.

REACH HARBOR

Drive up the road to the dead end and then get out.

Follow the road to the north until you reach a road block. Then get out and head up the dirt trail to the red smoke. There is a SCAR in a nearby shed if you want to pick it up. However, something with a bit more range and firepower is best.

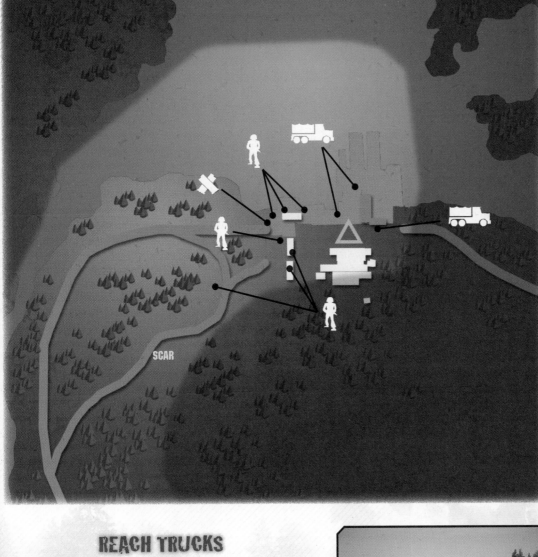

SCAR

REACH TRUCKS

The enemies below are sitting ducks waiting for you to kill them.

The squad has completed its objective of getting to the harbor. However, your squad sees mercenaries down below and hopes to find some gold as well. As a result, your new orders are to get to the trucks to get the gold. Rather than shooting all the enemies below and waiting for them to come after you, use the mortar strike designator to systematically destroy the base below, starting with the barracks. Some soldiers will make it out of the base, so fire your rifle or light machine gun to eliminate them. Once the base is clear, move in and make for the trucks.

Bombard the base with mortar strikes.

As you enter the base, the trucks drive off, getting away before you can take the gold they are carrying.

PRIMA Official Game Guide

BATTLEFIELD **BAD COMPANY**

Welcome · Basic Training · Infantry · Vehicles · Campaign · Multiplayer · Appendix

Welcome to Bad Company | Acta non Verba | Crossing Over | Par for the Course | Air Force One | Crash and Grab | Ghost Town

CROSSING OVER

After the mercenary trucks left the harbor, our squad decided to follow after them in the humvee. Unfortunately, the convoy of trucks carrying the gold crossed into Serdaristan—a neutral country. It looked like the gold was gone for good. Not known for his common sense or self-control, Haggard decided international law or foreign policy was not going to stop him from getting that gold. Without any warning, he took off running for the border and crossed into Serdaristan. Sarge was not happy at all. However, Haggard is part of our squad, so Sarge ordered us to go get Haggard before he got killed—or created an international incident. And that is how Bad Company invaded another country.

> Collectibles in this mission: 6
> Gold in this mission: 5

SAVING PRIVATE HAGGARD

STOP HAGGARD FROM INVADING A NEUTRAL COUNTRY.

➡ REACH HAGGARD BY THE SMOKE

REACH HAGGARD BY THE SMOKE

Target the soldiers in the towers.

As soon as the mission begins, your squad comes under fire from enemy soldiers at the border crossing. Crouch down and pull up your ironsights to begin clearing out the area below. Target the

Shoot at explosive barrels and crates to kill nearby enemies.

soldiers in the towers first. One of them mans a machine gun. Also watch out for a soldier who fires an RPG at you from the attic of a building. He can be hard to spot until he starts launching rockets at you. Finally, for soldiers on the ground, try shooting at explosive objects for quick kills—especially if the enemies are behind cover.

Once you clear out as many enemies as you can from your hilltop vantage point, head down to the road and search the two buildings at the entrance to the base. The northern building

Take out the RPG soldier in this attic.

contains a mortar strike designator while the southern bunker has an AN94 assault rifle—one of the collectibles you need to pick up. Put it back down and stick with the M416 for now.

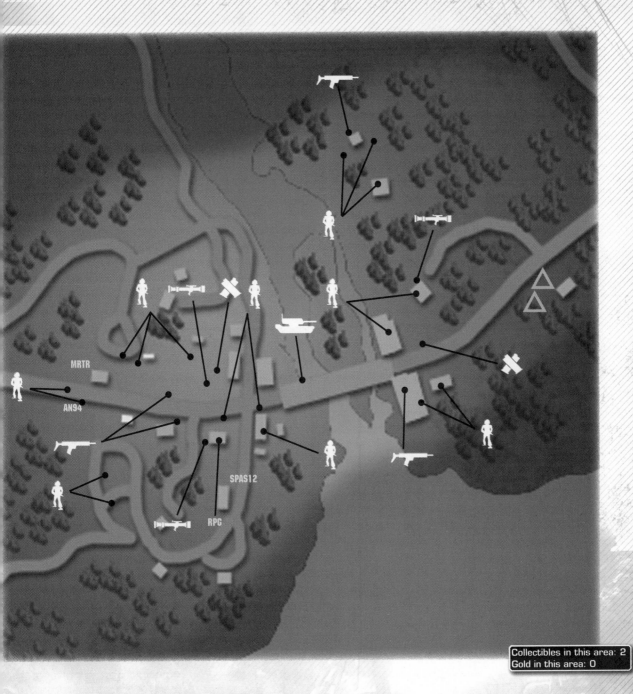

MRTR

AN94

SPAS12

RPG

Collectibles in this area: 2
Gold in this area: 0

Here comes the tank. The stationary missile launchers are a good way to destroy this threat.

As you enter the base, an enemy tank rolls down the street and begins firing on your squad. You have a few options for dealing with this tank. Since you picked up the mortar strike designator, you can call in artillery fire on the tank. However, you have to expose yourself for a few seconds to select the target. There are also a couple of stationary missile launchers located on each side of the street. A couple of missile hits and the tank will be destroyed. The final option is an RPG located in the

building south of the southern missile launcher. Pick it up and take cover behind sandbags or inside one of the buildings. As with the missile launcher, the RPG takes a couple hits to get a kill on the tank.

 **TIP**

While engaging the tank, other enemy soldiers may shoot at you. Be ready to pull out the auto injector and heal yourself while ducking behind cover. Then continue firing at the tank until it is destroyed. It is easy to be killed during this fight if you don't watch your health and heal early and often.

BAD COMPANY
BATTLEFIELD

Welcome • Basic Training • Infantry • Vehicles • Campaign • Multiplayer • Appendix

Welcome to Bad Company | Acta non Verba | **Crossing Over** | Par for the Course | Air Force One | Crash and Grab | Ghost Town

Watch for a couple soldiers in this house just east of the southern missile launcher. They fire out the windows while barely exposing themselves.

Use your grenade launcher or the missile launcher to blow away the walls along with the soldiers.

The enemy has positioned a machine gun on the opposite end of the bridge, a bit to the south. Call in a mortar strike to wipe out that threat. If you want, bombard all the buildings on the opposite side of the river

You can also wade across the river to the north of the bridge and avoid the machine gun.

to clear out as much resistance as possible before crossing. Another tactic is to forget the bridge and get your feet wet as you cross the river to the north of the bridge. Watch out for soldiers in the barracks on the other side as well as inside a bunker to the north of the barracks. Use your rifle to kill the enemies at a distance. Then move in to finish off any survivors. Stop by the ammo box to fill up before continuing on.

Don't forget to look for collectibles.

Clear out the rest of the base on this side of the river and restock at the ammo box. Also search a house in the southern part of this area to find a SPAS12 shotgun. Pick it up to earn the collectible, then get your M416, since you need some longer-range firepower for the rest of the mission. Next, head for the bridge crossing over the river.

The sign says Democratic Republic of Serdaristan. Whenever democratic and republic are both in a name of a country, the government is usually neither and the combined terms translate into "communist dictatorship".

Call in a mortar strike against the machine gun position on the opposite side of the river.

Continue down the road to meet up with the prodigal squad member. Haggard is patiently waiting for you by the smoke. However, he still wants to go after that gold.

Haggard is waiting by the smoke.

 ★ COVER YOUR TRACKS ★

COVER YOUR TRACKS BY DESTROYING THE HACKED COMMUNICATIONS ANTENNAS.

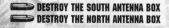 DESTROY THE SOUTH ANTENNA BOX   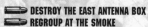 DESTROY THE EAST ANTENNA BOX
DESTROY THE NORTH ANTENNA BOX   REGROUP AT THE SMOKE

The end of the road to the northeast looks promising.

After meeting up with Haggard, Miss July informs you that Bad Company is in hot water for invading another country and is facing court martial. Since you are already in trouble, Sarge decides that you might as well get rich. However, before you can go after the gold, you need to destroy communications antennas so the Army can't track your position. Speaking of gold, take a look down the road to the northeast. At the end of the road you can see a mercenary sign. If the sign is there, gold is nearby.

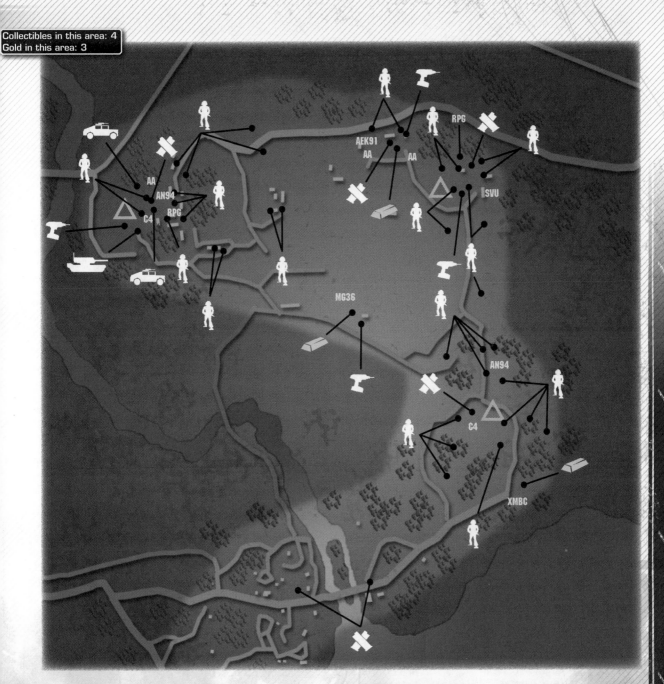

Collectibles in this area: 4
Gold in this area: 3

AEK91
AA
AA
RPG
SVU
AA
AN94
RPG
C4
MG36
AN94
C4
XMBC

The enemy has snipers positioned along the hills to the north.

As you move toward the mercenary sign, your squad comes under fire from snipers to the north. They are difficult to spot since they hide in the brush and trees. Be ready to heal since a sniper rifle can cause a lot of damage with a single shot. If you can see the snipers through your ironsights, try to shoot them. Another tactic, assuming you still have the mortar strike designator, is to target areas where the snipers are hiding. Even if you don't kill them outright, you take away their cover and concealment.

At the end of the road, pick up a collectible weapon and a gold bar.

Continue to the end of the road. There you can pick up a XM8C close assault rifle equipped with a silencer. However, it is best for short range combat, so take your M416 with you. Also open the mercenary case to take a gold bar.

PRIMA Official Game Guide

BAD COMPANY
BATTLEFIELD

Welcome · Basic Training · Infantry · Vehicles · Campaign · Multiplayer · Appendix

Welcome to Bad Company | Acta non Verba | **Crossing Over** | Par for the Course | Air Force One | Crash and Grab | Ghost Town

DESTROY THE SOUTH ANTENNA BOX

You need to destroy this antenna.

From the end of the road, head due north. This allows you to approach the objective while staying in cover. Watch out for more snipers. They are to the north of you as well as to the northwest near the antenna. Stay low as you advance and kill snipers as soon as you see them.

TIP

Pick up an SV98 from a dead sniper to earn another collectible. This can be a good weapon to take with you. The downside is that you don't have any grenades or a grenade launcher. However, you do have a pistol for dealing with enemies up close. While the rifle you pick up will probably not have much ammo, there is an ammo box near the antenna where you can fill up.

Clear out the barracks and surrounding area.

There are several soldiers near the antenna. Pick off some of them from a distance with either an assault rifle or a sniper rifle if you decided to swap. Continue to the objective and clear out the barracks and the area around the antenna so you can destroy it without being shot in the back. Inside the barracks find some C4. Pick it up and place a charge on the electrical box at the base of the antenna. Detonate it to complete the objective. Before leaving this area, be sure to visit the ammo box.

The charge is primed and ready to blow.

TIP

Another way to destroy this antenna, as well as the other two, is to call in mortar strikes on them. You can actually destroy the south antenna by targeting it from the end of the road where you find the gold. Use the mortar strike to clear out the area around the antenna as well. It won't destroy the ammo box, but it will kill soldiers.

DESTROY THE EAST ANTENNA BOX

A sniper is hiding in this building. Shoot him through the window.

Time to move on. Advance north toward a house. Stay in the cover to the east of the road and be ready to engage the enemy up ahead. A sniper waits inside the house, looking out through a window for targets. Use ironsights or the sniper rifle scope to take him out with a head shot. Then move into the house and get ready for a counter-attack. There is an AN94 assault rifle inside as well as the dead sniper's SV98. If you picked up the sniper rifle before, get the AN94 to deal with the soldiers that come at you from the north. You can always come back for the sniper rifle.

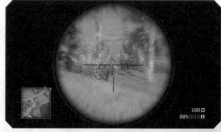

The sniper rifle is a great way to kill enemy snipers.

Continue advancing north, staying to the east of the road. As you get to the ridge where the road turns west, be ready to engage snipers to the north and west. After killing both snipers, keep going north.

Move across this field, using the concrete obstacles for cover.

Cross the open field, sprinting from one concrete obstacle to another for cover. You should be able to make it to the tree line without any resistance.

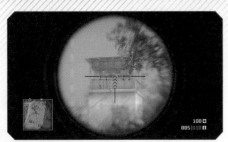

Shoot the soldier manning the machine gun in the tower near the east antenna.

Climb back down from the tower and get into the armored jeep. Drive toward the antenna and use the machine gun to kill any remaining enemies around the antenna. Then dismount and place a C4

Use the jeep to finish off enemies near the antenna.

charge on the antenna box if you still have explosives with you. Otherwise, destroy it using the nearby RPG, the machine gun on the vehicle, or even by calling in a mortar strike on the antenna.

As the alarm sounds at the base, pull back if you have the sniper rifle to engage enemies approaching from the direction of the antenna at long range.

The base to the north is guarded by a soldier in a tower manning a machine gun. Take aim and kill him while still at a distance. As you approach the base, an alarm sounds. Pull back to some cover and shoot at soldiers as they come at you or fire at you from behind sandbags. Stay put until all attackers have been neutralized, then advance on the base.

An enemy helicopter attacks after you destroy the second antenna.

Not long after the antenna comes crashing down, an enemy helicopter arrives and makes attack runs on your squad. Hop back into the armored jeep. One of your squad tells you to head to the barn. Drive out of the base and follow the road around to the right. The barn is located northwest of the base. As soon as you get to the barn, jump out and sprint to the AA gun. Start firing at the helicopter and shoot it down.

Watch for enemies hiding in the two barracks.

Get to the AA gun near the barn and shoot down the helicopter.

Pick up an SVU sniper rifle in the tower.

Though the base may seem quiet, there are still soldiers in the two barracks. Be ready to kill them. Don't blow up the explosive tank near the armored jeep, since you can use the jeep in a little bit. Your squad helps you clear the barracks. Then climb up the ladder to the tower and pick up an SVU sniper rifle. Though it takes two body shots to kill an enemy rather than the SV98's one shot, the SVU is semiautomatic with more ammunition. Try it out for now.

After the aerial threat is eliminated, clear out the enemies in this area. One soldier hides up in the loft of the barn and shoots down at you. Kill him, then the two soldiers in the house to the west. By this time, you might have noticed a mercenary sign near the AA gun. You know what that means. Head down to the garage under the barn to find a case with some gold for you to steal. If you want an assault rifle, there is an AEK91 in the house. A power tool can be found in the barn if you need to do some vehicle repairs. However, there is an armored jeep in the barn and another by the house, so it is easier to just get a new vehicle for your driving pleasure.

The race to the barn while the helicopter attacks can be stressful. If you want to take it easier, clear out the barn area with the AA guns before you destroy the antenna. Place a charge on the antenna box while you are there, but don't detonate it until you are by the AA gun. Another option is to call in a mortar strike on the antenna while at the barn. Then man the AA gun and wait for the helicopter to arrive.

PRIMA Official Game Guide

BATTLEFIELD BAD COMPANY

Welcome · Basic Training · Infantry · Vehicles · Campaign · Multiplayer · Appendix

Welcome to Bad Company | Acta non Verba | **Crossing Over** | Par for the Course | Air Force One | Crash and Grab | Ghost Town

Follow the roads south and then west to find this house off by itself.

Before you go after the next objective, take a side trip in your vehicle. The lone house you need to visit is due south of the barn. You can drive cross country to get there or follow the roads back to the base with the eastern antenna and then head south. Turn right at each intersection and you eventually reach this location. Luckily, it is deserted. However, the mercenary sign outside signifies there is gold on the inside. Pick up a bar as well as an MG36 to earn another collectible. This gives you a lot more firepower and this light machine gun also features a nice scope.

The mercenary sign is always a welcome sight.

Pick up some additional firepower.

DESTROY THE NORTH ANTENNA BOX

There is only one more antenna to destroy and there are a couple of different ways to accomplish this goal. The antenna is located in an enemy base that is well defended. The easiest way is to head east from the house

Watch out for snipers on the granary catwalks.

with the gold. You have to take a short drive cross country to get back onto a road leading to the base. As you drive past farms to your left, snipers may fire on you. There is no need to clear out these farms, so just keep driving east.

Destroy the enemy vehicle.

Race into the enemy base.

When you approach the base, an enemy armored jeep drives out to engage you. Switch to the gunner's seat and destroy the enemy with machine gun fire. Once it is destroyed, follow the road right into the base. Rather than approach cautiously, drive in at full speed.

Time to upgrade to a tank.

A tank is parked near this back entrance into the base. Stop right before you get to the tank, jump out of your vehicle, and hop into the tank. You begin in the driver's seat which also gives you command of the main gun. If you want to use the machine gun, switch to the gunner's seat. From its parked position, use the tank's weapons to clear out a lot of the enemies in this part of the base. Fire the main gun to blow holes in the buildings and expose the soldiers hiding inside. Then drive the tank to the east to clear out the rest of the base.

Along the northern road to the base, watch out for enemy soldiers, some of whom are armed with RPGs.

Another way to get to the base is to drive back north to the barn and then follow the northern road west toward the base. Soldiers wait near the road to ambush you with RPG and rifle fire. Kill them and keep going. As you get near the base, the armored jeep comes out to meet you. As with the previous strategy, switch to the gunner's seat and destroy the enemy vehicle. By the time you get into the base, your vehicle will be about ready to blow up. Jump out and take cover in the large garage in the southeast corner of the base where you can pick up an RPG.

Rush into the base from the north.

For a change, use the AA gun to destroy the antenna box.

All that remains is to destroy the antenna box. There are a number of ways to accomplish this. You can use an RPG, place a C4 charge on it, fire the tank's weapons, or even use the nearby AA gun.

Use your MG36 to kill soldiers in towers and around the base.

While staying behind cover as much as possible, begin clearing out the enemies. Advance cautiously toward the antenna along with your squad. There are soldiers hiding in most of the buildings, so be ready for ambushes. Pick up the RPG to blow holes in walls if needed, since these mercenary soldiers like to hide behind walls, pop up into a window to shoot at you, and duck back down again.

REGROUP AT THE SMOKE

After getting rid of the last antenna, meet up with your squad at the red smoke. From this position, you can see enemy trucks headed east. Sarge mentions there is a harbor in that direction, and that your squad should go after them.

The smoke is behind the destroyed antenna.

CHASE THE GOLD

 REACH THE HARBOR

MAP ON NEXT PAGE

Hop into the tank and exit the base.

IFVs take a couple hits to eliminate.

CHASE AFTER THE TRUCKS TO THE HARBOR.

REACH THE HARBOR

Armored jeeps only take a single hit to destroy with your tank's main gun.

Your next objective is to get to the harbor all the way to the east. You definitely need a tank to complete this part of the mission, so climb into the one by the antenna. It does not matter whether you exit out of the base through the north or south entrance. Be ready to engage lots of enemies. The first you run into either way are a couple of soldiers with RPGs. Your squad gunner can usually take care of them as you keep driving. The next threats to arrive are a couple of armored jeeps. Use your main gun to shoot these vehicles.

As you keep moving east, you come across more armored jeeps as well as IFVs and even other tanks. The best tactic is to keep moving to be a harder target for the enemy to hit. If necessary, stop to fire, then hit the gas and get moving again. IFVs can take a couple hits while other tanks require three or more hits. As your tank takes damage, hop out to repair it in between engagements.

Frequently take time to repair your tank.

PRIMA Official Game Guide

BAD COMPANY
BATTLEFIELD

Welcome · Basic Training · Infantry · Vehicles · Campaign · Multiplayer · Appendix

Welcome to Bad Company | Acta non Verba | **Crossing Over** | Par for the Course | Air Force One | Crash and Grab | Ghost Town

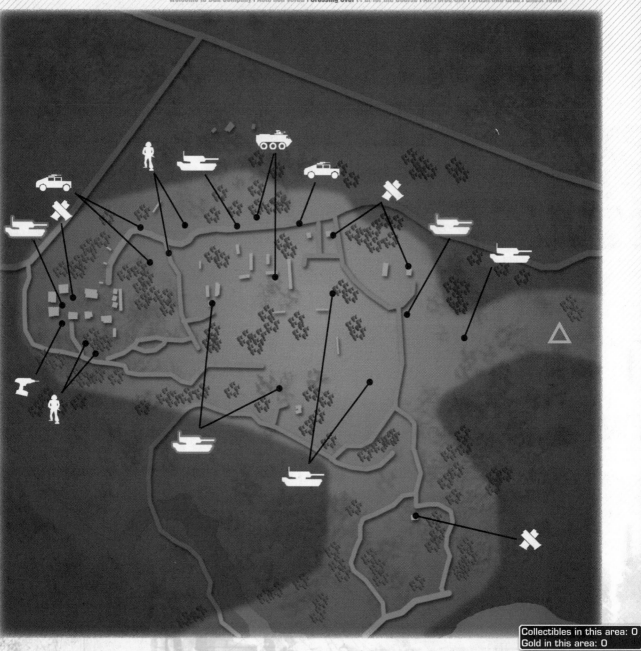

Collectibles in this area: 0
Gold in this area: 0

If you have to repair your tank during the middle of a fight, pop smoke to conceal your tank and then hop out to fix it. The smoke screen is only temporary, so get back in the tank quickly and be ready to continue the fight.

When fighting other tanks, try to keep moving and, if possible, hit them from the side or rear where their armor is thinner.

If your tank is destroyed, there are available tanks at some of the farms as well as the lone house where you found gold. Get to them and continue heading east. You encounter more tanks as you move through the open area with the concrete obstacles. Try to stay away from these obstacles since they limit your mobility. If you get stuck

Continue through the open area with the concrete obstacles.

on one, you are a sitting duck for the enemy tanks. Keep driving east through the valley until you reach the red smoke to complete your objective.

Drive to the red smoke.

LOCATE THE GOLD

FIGHT THROUGH THE HARBOR AND LOCATE THE GOLD.

🔫 SCOUT THE HARBOR   🔫 REACH THE CARGO SHIP

Collectibles in this area: 0
Gold in this area: 1

S20K

XMBC

AEK971

RPG

MRTR

SV98

PRIMA Official Game Guide

BAD COMPANY BATTLEFIELD

Welcome · Basic Training · Infantry · Vehicles · Campaign · Multiplayer · Appendix

Welcome to Bad Company | Acta non Verba | Crossing Over | Par for the Course | Air Force One | Crash and Grab | Ghost Town

You are fighting on foot again as you advance toward the harbor.

As you begin working toward your next objective, you have to leave the tank behind. While its firepower would come in handy, you need to move through tight spaces.

This tower contains a machine gun. Since you more than likely don't have an RPG, shoot the gunner to neutralize this threat.

SCOUT THE HARBOR

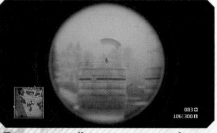

Try to neutralize as many enemies as possible from your starting position.

The combat begins right at the start of this part of the mission. There are several enemies on the fuel tanks and catwalks in front of you. Bring up your ironsights or scope and start picking them off one by one. Head north to the gate so you can enter the refinery area. Once inside, follow the fence line to the south.

Kill the armored jeep's gunner as well. See the case on top of the shipping containers? It sure looks like one of those cases the mercenaries keep their gold in.

As you get across the first pool, look for a tower to the southeast. It contains a machine gun that has a good field of fire to the catwalk over the next pool of water. Rather than let it kill you, shoot the gunner as soon as you can get him into your sights. An armored jeep also rolls into the area to the east of you. Again, take aim at and kill the soldier manning the machine gun, followed by other enemies that disembark. Shoot the explosive barrels to take out those on foot.

Climb up these stairs to the catwalks.

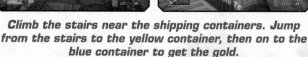

Climb the stairs near the shipping containers. Jump from the stairs to the yellow container, then on to the blue container to get the gold.

Advance along the catwalk across the second pool. If you want an S20K shotgun, there is one at the end of the catwalks. However, you are better off sticking with your current weapon. Rather than continuing on to the elevated area, climb down the stairs and move north toward the shipping containers. Climb up the first flight of stairs there, then jump from the stairs to the yellow container. Next, jump over to the blue container and open the case to steal another gold bar.

These metal plates on the sides of the catwalks offer good cover while engaging enemy soldiers.

Continue along the fence line until you come to stairs leading up to the catwalks. Since almost all of the enemies in this area are on the catwalks, you don't want to make an easy target at ground level. Take cover behind the metal plates on the catwalk and look for enemies up ahead. Engage as many as possible from a distance, then advance. Follow the catwalk to the east over a pool of water.

Another armored jeep arrives.

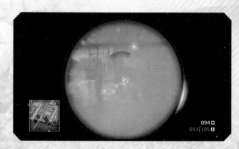

By now you probably need this ammo box located near the stairs.

Head back to the stairs and climb to the next level. You are starting in this area in the north and will work your way south, clearing as you go. Start with the large building near the stairs. As you kill enemies around it, another armored jeep will arrive. Take out the gunner and then go after other infantry in the area. Advance to the south to get to the ammo box for some much needed rearming.

To get to the next higher level which leads to the harbor, you can take the catwalk, drive a captured armored jeep up the ramp...

...or climb up these pipes in the south.

After getting some ammo, you have a choice of how to proceed. The most straightforward way to get to the next area is by following the catwalk toward the warehouse. Engage enemies along the way, including the soldier manning a machine gun in a tower to the south. Another option is to get into the armored jeep and drive it up a ramp to the south of the catwalk. This gives you some protection and heavier firepower as you clear out enemies in this next area. However, the best tactic is to keep moving south to a warehouse to find an RPG. Of course, you have to clear out this building first before waltzing in for a rocket launcher. Exit the building through the southern

doorways. It looks like your pathway is blocked by wire fences. Shoot the explosive crates by the fences to blast a way through. Climb up the large pipes, then jump up and over the concrete barrier at the top. This route helps you avoid being shot by all the enemies in the central part of this area.

Move into the warehouse near the top of the pipes, clear it out, and begin engaging enemies to the north. Some soldiers hide behind concrete barriers. With your RPG, take

Pick up this sniper rifle.

aim at the barrier and fire. Good-bye barrier and soldier. After eliminating all the soldiers you can from within the warehouse, move east into a barracks to pick up an SV98 sniper rifle. This comes in handy during the next part of this mission. You can also find a mortar strike designator in the warehouse to the north.

Call in mortar strikes to clear out remaining enemies.

Now that you have the mortar strike designator, call in some artillery strikes on the remaining enemies in this area. You can also snipe at them with your rifle. Once the area is all clear, continue to the red smoke to receive another objective.

Advance to this red smoke to complete your recon of the harbor.

PRIMA Official Game Guide

BAD COMPANY

BATTLEFIELD

Welcome · Basic Training · Infantry · Vehicles · Campaign · Multiplayer · Appendix

Welcome to Bad Company | Acta non Verba | Crossing Over | Par for the Course | Air Force One | Crash and Grab | Ghost Town

REACH THE CARGO SHIP

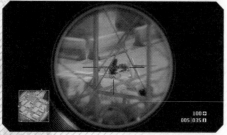

Collectibles in this area: 0
Gold in this area: 1

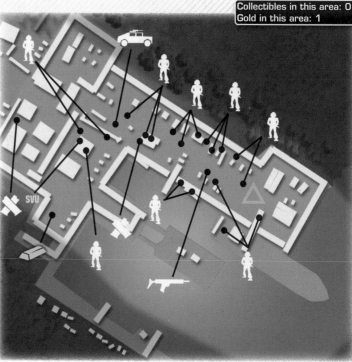

Snipe at the gunner in the armored jeep below as well as any other soldiers who try to man the machine gun.

This part of the mission allows you to get a lot of experience playing as a sniper if you choose. While you could also use an assault rifle with its grenade launcher, or a light machine gun, sniping is a good way to go. Move to the stairs and take cover behind sandbags. An armored jeep is parked below. Use your sniper rifle to kill the gunner with a single shot. Then engage any other nearby soldiers. Watch for one or two to try and get into the vehicle and operate the gun. You can also kill a soldier in the building next to the ammo box. He is standing next to a window. Shoot him now so you don't have to deal with him up close later.

Try to get them while you are on the catwalk. However, you will probably have to climb down the stairs to clear them out. Inside this building is an SVU sniper rifle. While it is faster to fire, it takes a couple hits to take out enemies. Go ahead and pick it up.

Enter this barracks at the southern end of the harbor to find the last gold bar in this mission.

Kill this sniper on the cargo ship before he even knows you are in the area.

Once you have shot all visible enemies, walk out onto the catwalk just until you see a sniper on the cargo ship. Kill him. Then check if you can see any enemies in the building down and to your right. There are two soldiers in there.

Continue heading south until you reach a green barracks. Walk on in and open a case to steal another gold bar. Now it is time to get back to the objective. There are a couple of ways you can get to the cargo ship. Either clear out the enemies along the main pier from a flanking position, or hit them head on with a direct assault. The flanking attack is much easier, but requires a sniper rifle. The direct assault can also use a sniper rifle, but an assault rifle is a better choice.

Shoot at enemies through the window. Use your pistol for fighting up close instead of your sniper rifle.

FLANKING ATTACK

From the southern pier, clear out most enemies who are waiting to ambush you before they detect you.

After exiting the barracks with the gold, head east toward the southern pier. There are concrete barriers to use for cover. From this position, shoot through the windows of the building by the ammo box and kill all soldiers inside. Continue moving down the pier to take out more soldiers among the shipping containers. While the SVU takes two or three body hits to eliminate enemies, you have the time for head shots which kill with a single hit.

Climb up onto this large pipe and walk along it to keep moving farther out toward the sea.

This soldier mans a machine gun on the main pier. However, if you kill him from the flank, you have eliminated a major threat when advancing along the main pier.

When the pier ends, climb up onto a large pipe and keep flanking the enemy on the main pier. By using this tactic, you can eliminate a vast majority of the enemies on the main pier. Be sure to watch for enemy snipers located up on top of structures on the main pier. They are your main threat. Once you have cleared out all the enemies you can see, jump down into the water and swim over to a ramp leading up to the main pier. If needed, head to the ammo box to restock for the final push.

DIRECT ASSAULT

Try using the armored jeep for an assault on the main pier.

Clear out the building by the ammo box.

If you have decided to go for the more direct approach, start off by making your way to the enemy armored jeep. Since you have already cleared it, you can hop in, start driving around, and use its machine gun to engage the enemy. However, the enemy can make short work of it as you drive down the pier. Therefore, it is best to go on foot. Start by clearing out the building by the ammo box. There will usually be one or two soldiers still inside.

Take out enemy snipers.

Mortars work great for destroying these barracks.

Now climb up the stairs onto the roof of the building you just cleared. From here, shoot at some enemy snipers positioned up on structures down toward the end of the pier. Stay low and try to kill any soldiers you can see walking near the shipping containers. Finally, call in mortar strikes on the barracks along the pier. It usually takes a couple bombardments to knock them down, but it also takes care of four soldiers hiding in these structures.

PRIMA Official Game Guide

BAD COMPANY
BATTLEFIELD

Welcome · Basic Training · Infantry · Vehicles · Campaign · Multiplayer · Appendix

Welcome to Bad Company | Acta non Verba | **Crossing Over** | Par for the Course | Air Force One | Crash and Grab | Ghost Town

Climb back down from the roof after you have caused as much death and destruction as possible. While you can follow the road down the pier, a machine gun covers this route. Therefore, walk along the southern side of

Watch out for soldiers waiting to ambush you as you walk by the shipping containers.

the main pier. There are several enemies in this area, so be ready to fight. Also watch for enemy snipers up high. Clear as you advance toward the end of the pier and your objective.

Make your way to the end of the pier.

Just as your squad is about the get a lot of gold, the U.S. Army arrives. Since you have cleared out all enemies between the border and the harbor, the Army was able to move on in, following your path of destruction. Illegal invasions are frowned upon by the military brass, so it seems like Bad Company is under arrest.

PAR FOR THE COURSE

Collectibles in this mission: 8
Gold in this mission: 5

The Army arrested Bad Company for their illegal invasion—although the charges were for going AWOL. However, since the brass is concerned about Serdaristan and its leader, they have made a deal with me. Since my squad is already considered AWOL, I have been ordered back into Serdaristan to see what I can learn. Though this country is supposedly neutral, it seems like the leader has been playing sides—and not the side of the U.S. Therefore, thanks to Haggard's momentary—who are we kidding, it is all the time—lack of judgement, Bad Company has provided the Army with deniability. However, if I do my job, all will be forgiven.

★ REACH THE VISTA POINT ★

GET UP TO THE OBSERVATION POINT AND SCOUT THE TERRAIN AHEAD.

▸ REGROUP AT THE SMOKE

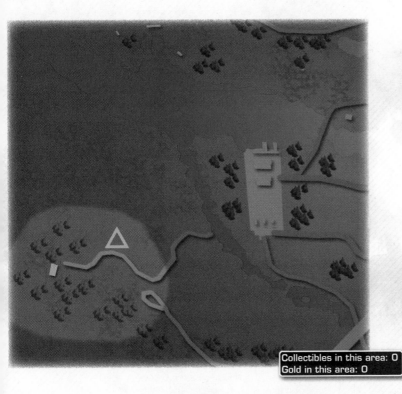

Collectibles in this area: 0
Gold in this area: 0

REGROUP AT THE SMOKE

Move out soldier!

The red smoke is at the observation point. Note the "No Photo" sign. What are they afraid you might take a picture of?

While none of your squad are happy about this mission, it does offer a way out of Bad Company. Luckily, this first objective is merely a hike—and not even all that taxing. Follow the path to an observation point from which you can scout out the surrounding terrain. Walk to the red smoke to get your new orders.

PRIMA Official Game Guide

BAD COMPANY
BATTLEFIELD

Welcome · Basic Training · Infantry · Vehicles · Campaign · Multiplayer · Appendix

Welcome to Bad Company | Acta non Verba | Crossing Over | **Par for the Course** | Air Force One | Crash and Grab | Ghost Town

★ DESTROY THE MISSILE LAUNCHERS ★

DESTROY THE ANTI-AIRCRAFT MISSILES TO SECURE A SAFE EXTRACTION.

- DESTROY THE SOUTH MISSILE LAUNCHER
- DESTROY THE EAST MISSILE LAUNCHER
- DESTROY THE WEST MISSILE LAUNCHER
- REGROUP AT THE SMOKE

Collectibles in this area: 5
Gold in this area: 2

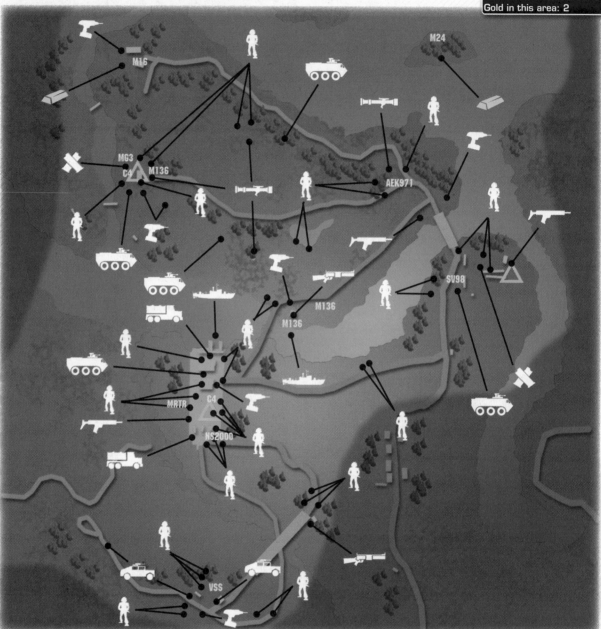

There goes your ride home.

The helicopter which dropped off the squad flies out over the military bases below. It is performing a recon under the guise of a search and recover mission. However, it quickly comes under fire and is shot down. It seems that Serdaristan is no longer neutral. Now you have no restrictions on violence.

Before leaving the observation area, take a look at the terrain up ahead along with your mission map. Try to correlate what you see with what is on the map. This will help you prepare for possible engagements.

This bridge looks like it has a tower at one end—with weapons for preventing a crossing.

Now head down the trail to the southeast to find some transportation, since you have a lot of ground to cover to get to your objectives.

This armored jeep is just sitting here with no one around. Go ahead and borrow it.

As you are walking down the trail, don't turn with it to the left. Instead, keep going straight ahead and come across an armored jeep. There are no soldiers guarding it, so hop in and start driving down the road to the southeast. As you approach some houses, be ready for action.

Shoot the enemy armored jeep first.

Use rocks for cover as you assault the southern house.

As you approach the houses, an enemy armored jeep opens fire. Switch to the gunner's seat and destroy it. The other threats in this area are the soldiers armed with RPGs. Try to shoot them as well. However, if your vehicle takes more than fifty percent damage, jump out and move in on foot to prevent being killed when the vehicle is destroyed by enemy fire. Start clearing out the house to the south and on your right. Sprint up to the rocks in front of the house and crouch down behind them for cover. There are a couple soldiers inside. Launch a grenade or two to blow them up or at least blast a hole in the wall so the enemies are easier to hit. Once the house is clear, move into it and use it for cover.

Go ahead and launch grenades and use a lot of ammo while clearing out this area. While there is not an ammo box here, you can pick up ammo from the assault rifles dropped by the enemy soldiers.

There are more soldiers in the northern house.

Pick up a VSS sniper rifle for a collectible.

From the southern house, you have a clear field of fire to the northern house. There are at least a couple soldiers in there, so use grenades to blow out the walls, then shoot the enemies and clear out this second building. Pick up a power tool near the southern house, then walk over to the northern house to find a VSS sniper rifle. Not only is this a collectible, you can actually use it to make the next part of this mission a bit easier.

Use the VSS to clear out the tower on the other side of the bridge.

Exit the house and head north to a position with a good view of the nearby bridge. The tower on the opposite side contains an automatic grenade launcher. Bring up your scope and shoot the gunner in the tower. Also try to pick off as many soldiers near the tower as you can. Some are armed with RPGs which can really make a bridge crossing difficult. After killing as many enemies as possible, head back to the house and retrieve your M416. Climb into the nearby armored jeep, then start driving across the bridge.

Instead of driving across the bridge right away, follow the road that leads under the bridge. You encounter a couple soldiers. One of them is carrying a PKM light machine gun. Kill him and pick up the weapon to earn another collectible. If you don't get it now, there is another near the end of the mission.

PRIMA Official Game Guide

BAD COMPANY BATTLEFIELD

Welcome · Basic Training · Infantry · Vehicles · Campaign · Multiplayer · Appendix

Welcome to Bad Company | Acta non Verba | Crossing Over | **Par for the Course** | Air Force One | Crash and Grab | Ghost Town

Drive across the bridge, ready for trouble. Soldiers with RPGs may be waiting to ambush you.

As you approach the opposite side of the bridge, be ready for action. A few soldiers may have hidden during your sniping and are waiting to hit you with RPGs up close. Either run them over with the armored jeep or switch to the gunner's seat and mow them down. After the area around the tower is clear, dismount and repair the vehicle if you took any damage.

DESTROY THE SOUTH MISSILE LAUNCHER

Clear out the tower before crashing your way into the base.

Follow the road leading from the bridge to the base where the south missile launcher is located. As you get the tower in sight, switch to the gunner's seat and kill the soldier in the tower. Get back into the drivers seat and crash through the gate to enter the base. Turn to the right so you are facing north and either let your squad engage the enemies or take control of the machine gun to clear out the tower with the mounted machine gun and the soldiers in the barracks. Use the vehicle as long as you can, then dismount before it is destroyed.

Sarge mows down enemies as you drive.

Fire grenades at the barracks to get rid of the soldiers inside.

Since you can't kill all the enemies while inside the vehicle, get out and use your grenade launcher to punch holes into the walls of the barracks and then finish off any survivors. Next, clear out the concrete building with the missile launcher on top. Fire at the soldiers inside or launch grenades through the windows. After you have cleared out this part of the base, pick up an NS2000 in the southernmost barracks to earn another collectible, then take your assault rifle with you. You can also find a mortar strike designator and C4.

Clear out the motor pool next.

Before you destroy the missile launcher, make sure all enemies in the motor pool area to the north are neutralized. Shoot at the explosive tank along the wall to blow a hole in the side of the building, then move in to clear it out. Once the first building is clear, repeat the process with the second building. Use a grenade to blow a hole in the side wall this time.

Blow up the missile launcher to complete an objective.

Now that the base is completely clear, pick up the C4, climb the stairs to the roof, and place a charge on the launcher. Detonate it to complete the objective. However, before you stop to take a breather, get ready for a counterattack. An armored jeep drives up and stops near the motor pool buildings. While the gunner fires on your squad, other soldiers dismount and add to the attack. Take aim at the gunner and shoot him to silence the machine gun. Then finish off the rest of the enemies. This base is finally secure. Visit the ammo box to restock and get ready to go after the next objective. Also be sure to pick up the item you want to take along. There is a power tool in the motor pool. You can also choose from the C4 or the mortar strike designator. If you are not sure, the power tool can come in handy to repair your vehicle while the mortar strike designator is great for clearing out enemy defenses.

Focus on the gunner in the armored jeep.

primagames.com

DESTROY THE WEST MISSILE LAUNCHER

The decision—the IFV or the boat.

As you approach the west missile launcher, move in on foot to engage the rocket launcher and soldiers in the area.

The west missile launcher is on the large island to the north of your present location. You have two options for going after it. The motor pool offers both an IFV and a patrol boat. If you just want to go after the objectives and not worry about fighting enemy armor, take the boat. Otherwise, go with the IFV.

Due to the terrain around it, the west missile launcher base is tough to drive into with a vehicle. Therefore, go in on foot. Kill the soldier manning the rocket launcher and then approach from the south, using trees and the lay of the land for cover. In addition to soldiers wandering around the base, there are also some in the barracks. Launch a few grenades to clear the barracks out. Once it is clear, move in to find a power tool, an M136 rocket launcher, some C4, and an MG3 light machine gun. Pick up the latter to add it to your collectibles, then destroy the missile launcher. Try firing an M136 rocket at it. One hit will do the job.

Since both of the remaining two missile launchers are located near the water, you can use the patrol boat's grenade launchers to destroy them. In addition, you can also leave the boat along a shore and do some exploring on foot.

Whether you decide to take the IFV or boat, it is a good idea to eliminate the soldiers guarding the ford to the island. Take the IFV down the road, then get out before you arrive at the ford. Continue on foot

Dismount to destroy the enemy defenses at the ford.

to clear out the area before bringing the IFV across. Use your assault rifle to kill the soldier manning the automatic grenade launcher as well as the soldier with the RPG. Near the grenade launcher, you can find a power tool and an M136 rocket launcher. If you are going to take along the IFV, get the M136. For boat transportation, keep the mortar strike designator.

Another missile launcher destroyed.

When using the boat to get around, try calling in mortar strikes on the missile bases.

If you have chosen the naval approach, drive the patrol boat around the western side of the island and get off on the little island to the west. From here, walk north until you have a view of the barracks and base. Use the mortar strike designator to call in an artillery strike on the base. Two or three strikes in different locations should do the job. Then get back into your boat and drive it next to the base to get out and pick up some goodies.

Get ready for armored combat on the gold course.

The large island has rocket launchers and IFVs in the interior to help defend it against an armored attack. At times, it is best to dismount from your IFV and use the rocket launcher to take out enemy vehicles—or bring along a power tool and repair as needed. Use your rifle to kill the soldiers manning rocket launchers or carrying RPGs. Once you have taken out the main threats, get back into the IFV and start rolling again.

There is nobody here, but you can find some good stuff.

PRIMA Official Game Guide

BATTLEFIELD BAD COMPANY

Welcome · Basic Training · Infantry · Vehicles · Campaign · Multiplayer · Appendix

Welcome to Bad Company | Acta non Verba | Crossing Over | **Par for the Course** | Air Force One | Crash and Grab | Ghost Town

After taking care of the west launcher, head north either by land or water. There is a small base with a couple barracks. It is deserted, so walk right in. In one of the

Another case with a gold bar.

barracks you find an M16. Pick it up since it is a collectable and keep it. In the other barracks, steal another gold bar from the mercenaries. A road leads from this base to the east missile launcher. If you choose to follow it, you have to deal with another IFV as well as rocket launchers and infantry. Therefore, it is a better idea to head back to the ford in the south since you need to get a boat for the next part of the mission.

Take care of your IFV or you end up riding around in a golf cart.

DESTROY THE EAST MISSILE LAUNCHER

Take a boat to the small island in the northeast to find some gold and an M24 sniper rifle.

While you can assault the east missile launcher base from the ground by either crossing the bridge or working your way east from the ford, it is very difficult to get a vehicle into the base due to concrete barriers. In addition, most defenses are positioned to cover attacks from the road. Try surprising the enemy from the water. If you don't already have a boat, get one. Drive it clockwise around the large central island past the western side of the island. Make a short stop at the small island in the northeast where you can find some gold and a sniper rifle collectible. Pick up the M24, but then put it back down and keep using the M16.

Approach the last missile launcher from the north.

Call in a mortar strike to destroy the missile launcher.

As you approach the last base, you may have to take out an enemy patrol boat. Once the waters are clear, park the boat along the shore east of the missile launcher. Get out and move to a position from which you can call in a couple mortar strikes. The missile launcher should be destroyed as well as most of the defenders. Move in to finish off any survivors.

REGROUP AT THE SMOKE

Advance west across the missile launcher base to the red smoke to regroup with your squad and await new orders. There may still be enemies in the area, so move with caution and

Head to the smoke.

be ready to fight. Near the smoke is an SV98 sniper rifle and an IFV.

REACH AND PICK UP SUPPLIES ★ DESTROY THE TANK ★ REGROUP AT THE SMOKE

Collectibles in this area: 0
Gold in this area: 0

REACH AND PICK UP SUPPLIES

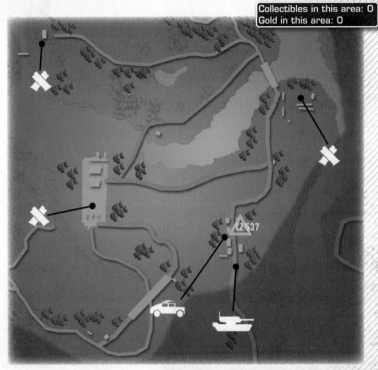

Drive the IFV to the next objective area.

Bad Company has eliminated all of the anti-aircraft missile launchers in the area. However, the Army is not able to send in an extraction helicopter at this time. To make up for this, Miss July, your radio contact, has arranged a surprise to be air dropped for you. Rather than walking, get into the IFV to the west of the base you just cleared. There is an SV98 sniper rifle nearby, but leave it behind and hold on to your M16. Drive the IFV along the roads to the objective area where an LZ-537 laser designator is waiting for you. Pick it up to complete the objective.

Pick up the laser designator.

DESTROY THE TANK

Hold the tank in your sights to designate it.

Just after you pick up the LZ-537, a tank rolls toward you from the south. Quickly take cover, then zoom in on the tank with the laser designator. Hold down the fire button to lock in the target. Once it is locked, continue to hold down the zoom button while steering the bomb toward the tank using the right stick. This can be tougher than it looks, so be ready to try again if you miss the first time.

Steer the bomb onto the target.

CAUTION ★ ★ ★

While you are trying to lock on to the tank, the tank will be firing at you. Therefore, keep an eye on your health. You may have to break the process before you get a lock to heal yourself. If possible, put a building between you and the tank. All you have to lock on to is just part of the tank. You can then guide the bomb in for a hit. After taking out the tank, practice the process some more. You can only laser target a vehicle. However, once the bomb is dropped, steer it wherever you want.

PRIMA Official Game Guide

BATTLEFIELD BAD COMPANY

Welcome · Basic Training · Infantry · Vehicles · Campaign · Multiplayer · Appendix

Welcome to Bad Company | Acta non Verba | Crossing Over | **Par for the Course** | Air Force One | Crash and Grab | Ghost Town

REGROUP AT THE SMOKE

Once you destroy the tank and feel comfortable with guiding in aerial bombardments, make your way to the red smoke to meet up with your squad to receive new orders.

Another reunion at the red smoke.

REACH THE SUPPLY STATION

ARM YOURSELF BEFORE THE ASSAULT ON THE PALACE.

ELIMINATE ALL ENEMIES

ELIMINATE ALL ENEMIES

Drive along the road until you can see and take out the machine gun in the tower up ahead.

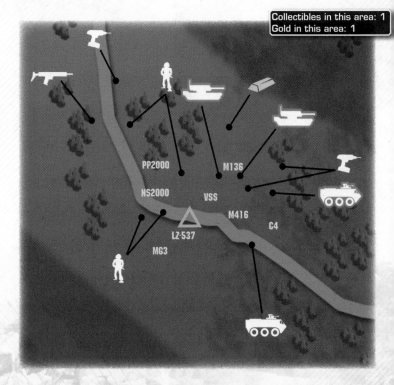

Collectibles in this area: 1
Gold in this area: 1

PP2000

NS2000

M136

VSS

LZ-S37

MG3

M416

C4

Load the squad back into the IFV and start rolling south down the road. It seems like you have a fight coming up at the palace. Therefore, you need to pick up some weapons at a supply station. Unfortunately, this station is well defended by the enemy. Continue down the road until you see a tower in the distance. Switch to the weapon's view and take out the soldier manning the gun. Once the tower is neutralized, move on toward the supply station and be ready for a fight.

Blast away at the enemy IFV before it destroys your vehicle.

As you search around the area, be sure to pick up the PP2000 to add to your collectibles.

Use the IFV's cannon to attack infantry hiding in the barracks and buildings from a distance before they can start shooting at you. As soon as you get to the left turn in the road, be ready to start firing at an enemy IFV coming toward you. Keep firing and destroy the enemy vehicle as quickly as possible. Then take out the soldier in the tower at the other side of the supply station area. After clearing out the soldiers you can get with the vehicle's guns, dismount and move into the buildings to clear them out and pick up any weapons you might need. Don't forget to collect the PP2000 which is in one of the barracks. An assault rifle, light machine gun, or even a sniper rifle, are good choices for the rest of this mission. What you take basically depends on your combat style.

The supply station also features a couple tanks as well as small arms.

A gold bar can be found to the north of the tanks.

There are a few vehicles parked at the eastern end of the supply station including two tanks and an IFV. If there are tanks, you know that you probably need their firepower for later in the mission. However, before hot wiring one, blow a hole in the fence behind them and walk north toward a monument where you find a mercenary case with a gold bar inside. Pick it up, then head back to the tanks and climb in one of them.

REACH THE PALACE

FIGHT YOUR WAY TO THE PRESIDENTIAL PALACE.

▶ REGROUP AT THE SMOKE

REGROUP AT THE SMOKE

Destroy the armored jeep by the bridge.

Cross the bridge and be ready for more enemies on the other side.

Drive your tank east out of the supply station and follow the road around to the north. As you approach the bridge, an enemy armored jeep blocks your way. One shot from your tank's main gun eliminates that threat. Keep rolling right across the bridge and be ready for another armored jeep. Another good shot and another enemy vehicle is left behind as a smoking wreck. After destroying this vehicle, you have a choice to make. If you

head due north, leaving the road and driving your tank across the golf course, you come to a monument where you can find a power tool and an M16. On the other hand, if you follow the road, you drive past a small enemy base where you can also find a power tool as well as a tank, IFV, and even a couple MG3 light machine guns. No matter which way you choose, you have to fight IFVs and tanks.

When engaging an enemy vehicle such as an IFV or tank, keep moving toward the target, but at an angle. The closer you get, the more accurate your shots will be. By not driving directly at the target, you make it harder for the enemy to hit you.

Find an M16 and a power tool at this monument.

PRIMA Official Game Guide

BATTLEFIELD BAD COMPANY

Welcome · Basic Training · Infantry · Vehicles · Campaign · Multiplayer · Appendix

Welcome to Bad Company | Acta non Verba | Crossing Over | **Par for the Course** | Air Force One | Crash and Grab | Ghost Town

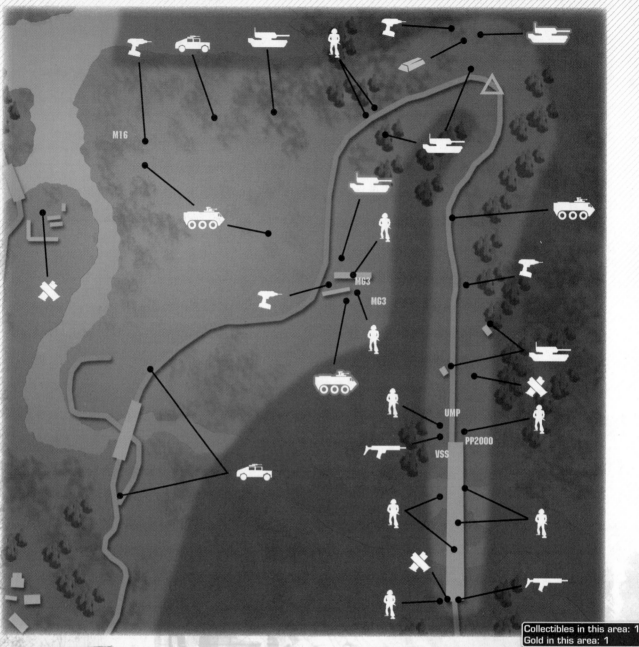

Collectibles in this area: 1
Gold in this area: 1

★ **TIP** ★

If possible, try to hit enemy tanks from the side or rear. The best way to do that is to drive around or past them. When dealing with tanks and infantry at the same time, shoot at the tank with the main gun first, then switch seats to use the machine gun to mow down the infantry.

Pick up a new tank at this small base alongside the road.

While you can repair your tank with a power tool, you can also pick up new tanks in a couple spots on the way to the palace. There is a small base next to the main road. A couple soldiers in the buildings are the only defenses here. Though there is an IFV here, stick with the greater firepower of the tank. As you get near the northern part of the map where the road turns to the east, be ready for another tank to appear. Keep moving and use the same tactics as before. If you take too much damage and need to repair, pop smoke before climbing out and using your power tool.

The fourth gold bar is located in the northeastern corner of the map.

Once you reach the northeastern corner of the map, where the road takes a turn to the south, turn your tank north and head off road to reach another mercenary case containing a gold bar. There is also a power tool nearby as well as a new tank. Repair your tank and leave the spare there in case you need to come back for it later. Climb into the tank and follow the road to the south.

A couple shots destroys the IFV on the road.

This tank to the east of the road is dug in, making it more difficult to hit.

Along the road, you engage an enemy IFV. Keep rolling and fire a couple of rounds into this vehicle to destroy it. However, once it is a smoking wreck, stop to repair any damage to your vehicle and get ready for a big fight. There are two tanks to the south—one to the east of the road and one right next to the road on the western side. Both of these tanks are partially dug in, making them difficult to destroy, so get in close. Charge the eastern tank first to destroy it. Keep moving since two tanks are firing at you. As soon as the first tank is destroyed, pop smoke and repair your tank. Then go after the tank on the western side of the road. If you lose your tank, hike back up north to pick up a new one.

A UMP can be found in the machine gun tower along the road.

Be sure to pick up the UMP submachine gun in the ground floor of the tower. Don't keep it, but add it to your collectibles. From this point on, you have to go on foot.

Aim at the soldier behind the machine gun shield to silence these threats.

Watch for soldiers on the upper and lower catwalks on either side of the bridge.

After destroying both tanks, keep moving south. Take out the machine gun tower right next to the road and use both the main gun and machine gun to clear out the barracks of all enemy soldiers.

The palace is on the other side of a long bridge. As you step on the bridge, explosions rack the structure and take out huge chunks of roadway. The only way across now is along catwalks to either side. If you don't already have a sniper rifle, pick up the VSS at the northern end of the bridge. This sniper rifle helps you survive the bridge crossing. The enemy has positioned a machine gun at the southern end of the bridge. A shield protects the gunner. However, with the VSS, you can fire through the slits in the shield to kill the gunner on the other side. Once the machine gun is silenced, start picking off soldiers along the catwalks. There are high and low catwalks on both sides of the bridge, so watch for enemies everywhere. Enemy soldiers like to hide on the lower levels and shoot up at you through the stairs, which makes it hard to see where the shots are coming from. Continue to advance, stopping behind steel plates on the railings for protection from enemy fire. Reach the red smoke to receive your next orders.

Push all the way across the bridge and meet up at the red smoke.

Welcome · Basic Training · Infantry · Vehicles · Campaign · Multiplayer · Appendix

Welcome to Bad Company | Acta non Verba | Crossing Over | **Par for the Course** | Air Force One | Crash and Grab | Ghost Town

CAPTURE THE PRESIDENT

KIDNAP PRESIDENT SERDAR.

▸ **REACH AND SECURE THE PALACE**   ▸ **REGROUP AT THE PALACE VAULT**

REACH AND SECURE THE PALACE

Top off your ammo by the barracks before approaching the palace.

As you enter the palace grounds, be ready for a major fight.

| Collectibles in this area: 1 |
| Gold in this area: 1 |

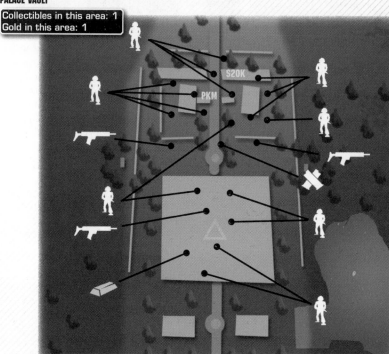

Your new orders are to enter the palace and kidnap President Serdar. This won't be easy. The palace is surrounded by mercenaries. Restock at the ammo box by the bridge before walking up the pathway to the palace. As soon as you approach the palace yard, get ready with your weapons. A couple of soldiers usually attack you right near the entrance. After killing them, sprint into the grounds and take cover behind the low concrete walls. The best position is either the northeastern or northwestern corners so you don't have to worry about being surrounded by enemies.

The grounds in front of the palace are crawling with mercenaries. There are also two machine guns at the southern end of the grounds. Try to silence them as quickly as possible by aiming through the slits in their shields. With all of the bullets in the air, expect to take a lot of hits. Be quick to duck down behind cover to heal. Before popping back up, use the minimap to line up your next target. That saves you vital time in acquiring a target for your shots.

Use the sniper rifle to take out the machine guns next to the palace.

The PKM light machine gun is located at the foot of the presidential statue. This gives you a lot more firepower for finishing up the mission.

Stay low behind the walls while healing and reloading, then pop up to take shots.

primagames.com

As the grounds clear out a bit, sprint to the foot of the statue and pick up a PKM light machine gun. This is the last collectible on the map. In addition, this weapon puts out a lot of firepower. Advance down one side of the grounds, clearing enemies as you go. Once you get to the palace, don't go in through the front doors. The enemy has a machine gun positioned inside to mow down anyone coming through the front. Instead, walk around to the back of the palace and come in the rear entrance after killing any enemies in this back area.

Enter through the back door and start clearing out enemies inside the palace.

A case with a gold bar can be found near the rear entrance on the western side of the room.

As soon as you enter the palace, watch out for enemies hiding around the corners of walls. Throw grenades around the enemies' cover to kill them. Also be sure to pick up the last gold bar from a case near the rear entrance. Clear out any enemies in the front room, however don't enter the room if you can help it, since enemies on the second floor will shoot down on you.

Clear out the second floor of enemies as well.

There are two staircases that lead up to the second floor from the front room as well as one staircase on each side of the palace which also lead up. Since the front room staircases are covered by the enemy, use one of the side staircases to get to the second floor and then begin clearing it out of all enemies. They will be hiding behind cover, so use the minimap to help detect and target them.

REGROUP AT THE PALACE VAULT

After all mercenaries around and inside the palace have been killed, you are ordered to move to the doors to the palace vault. This is on the second floor of the palace. Once you enter, the final objective is completed.

Move to these doors in the middle of the second floor.

Bad Company rushes in to capture President Serdar.

Sarge learns that your orders to capture the president have been changed. There is no evacuation chopper on its way. The Army has decided to go with deniability and leave your squad to fend for itself. This does not look good.

Fortunately, President Serdar has a way out for you. He is essentially a hostage to the mercenaries. If you will help him go into exile, he will help you get out of his country. The president offers his private helicopter for all of you to make your escape. It looks like you will be doing the flying.

PRIMA Official Game Guide

BAD COMPANY BATTLEFIELD

Welcome · Basic Training · Infantry · Vehicles · Campaign · Multiplayer · Appendix

Welcome to Bad Company | Acta non Verba | Crossing Over | Par for the Course | **Air Force One** | Crash and Grab | Ghost Town

AIR FORCE ONE

Collectibles in this mission: 0
Gold in this mission: 5

After having been abandoned by the Army in Serdaristan, our squad has managed to hook up with the former president of this country. In exchange for escorting him into exile, the ex-president is providing us with a ride out. It's not every day I get to ride in a pimped out helicopter gunship. I'm the pilot, since I'm are the only member of the squad with experience flying a helicopter. It's up to me to get the chopper and everyone in it safely across the border and out of Serdaristan.

★ HELICOPTER TUTORIAL ★

BRUSH UP ON YOUR HELICOPTER SKILLS. FOLLOW THE INSTRUCTIONS AND RULE THE SKY!

▭ LAND THE HELICOPTER   ▭ GET BACK TO AND REPAIR THE HELICOPTER   ▭ TAKE OFF AND DESTROY THE TRUCKS

LAND THE HELICOPTER

Collectibles in this area: 0
Gold in this area: 0

Practice flying the helicopter now before people start shooting at you.

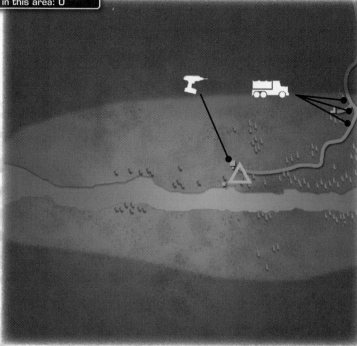

You are already airborne when the mission begins. The entire objective for now is to master the art of rotary winged flight. While flying a helicopter is not difficult, it is a bit different than driving a tank or boat since now you have to deal with altitude and pitch as well. The right control stick controls pitch and yaw. In other words, it tilts the nose of the aircraft up and down as well as rotates the chopper to the left and right. Think of this as your view when on foot. The left control stick controls your movement. Up and down make the helicopter move forward or backward while left and right cause the aircraft to slip to the left or right while maintaining the same facing—just like strafing while on foot. If you think of flying the helicopter just like moving around on foot, the process becomes very familiar. Use the left control stick for moving and the right control stick for controlling direction and aiming. The final controls let you adjust your altitude. These can vary depending on what platform you are playing—but one button increases your altitude while the other decreases it.

★ TIP ★

While you can customize the controls to your liking, the default settings are good as is. The only thing you might consider changing is inverting the vertical flight axis. This makes it easier to engage enemies while in targeting view since pushing up on the right stick will make the reticle go up.

Try out the targeting view.

Set down on a flat spot of open ground.

Before taking the helicopter in for a landing, try flying around the area. Toggle the camera button to switch between an external view, behind the chopper view, and the targeting view. The external view is best for flying around since you get a better view of the surrounding terrain. However, if you want to hit a target with your weapons, the targeting view shows where the weapons are aimed. After trying out the controls until you are comfortable, fly toward the objective icon. Position the helicopter right over the open area near the house and stop all horizontal motion. Then press the decrease altitude button until the helicopter has touched down on terra firma.

GET BACK TO AND REPAIR THE HELICOPTER

Pick up a power tool in this house.

Once you are on the ground, press the enter/exit button to disembark from the helicopter. Walk into the nearby house and locate a power tool. Pick it up, and then return to the helicopter.

Use the power tool to repair the damage and make the helicopter just like new. Now climb back into the pilot's seat.

Get back to the helicopter and fix it just like you would any other vehicle.

TAKE OFF AND DESTROY THE TRUCKS

Look for the red diamonds on the screen. They show the location of enemy vehicles.

Press the increase altitude button to get the helicopter back up into the air. Follow the road to the east to get to your next objective. Three trucks are approaching from the north. Once your helicopter's targeting computer detects them, red diamonds will appear on the screen to help you locate them. The helicopter is armed with two different types of weapons. When in the pilot's seat, you can fire rockets. These are not guided missiles and only fly in a straight line—right where you aim them. Hold down the fire button to fire off a continuous volley of rockets. These rockets are great for destroying buildings and enemy vehicles. The second weapon is the auto cannon which is positioned in a turret at the front of the helicopter. Haggard has control of the cannon and will automatically fire at enemies within range. Switch to the targeting view and then steer the helicopter so an enemy truck is right in the

Use the targeting view when firing rockets.

PRIMA Official Game Guide

BATTLEFIELD BAD COMPANY

Welcome · Basic Training · Infantry · Vehicles · Campaign · Multiplayer · Appendix

Welcome to Bad Company | Acta non Verba | Crossing Over | Par for the Course | **Air Force One** | Crash and Grab | Ghost Town

middle of the aiming reticle. Fire away and watch your rockets fly toward their target. Since it takes a short amount of time to get to the target, in order to hit these moving trucks, you need to aim a bit in front of the truck, leading it so that by the time the rocket travels the distance, the truck will have moved right into the path of the rocket.

Destroy two of the trucks with your rockets. Then press the switch seats button. While you don't really change seats with Haggard, you take control of the auto

Take control of the auto cannon.

cannon while Haggard holds the helicopter in a hover. As with rockets, use the targeting view when firing the cannon. Remember that while you control the cannon, the helicopter is hovering in one place. You can rotate the helicopter just by moving your view left and right. However, all forward and backward motion comes to a stop. Though the trucks can't fire back at you, remember to quickly use the cannons during actual combat and then return to the pilot's control so you can get the helicopter moving again. Otherwise, you are an easy target for the enemy. Use the cannon to destroy the last truck to complete your training.

MOVE OUT

 CONTINUE DOWN THE RIVER.

 FOLLOW THE RIVER

FOLLOW THE RIVER

Practice flying low, which makes it harder for the enemy to hit you since you can use the trees for cover.

Fly the helicopter east through the river valley. As you approach a house on the left bank of the river, a couple red triangles appear on the screen. Two enemy patrol boats are headed your way. Switch to targeting view and then begin firing rockets at these two targets. Use the right control stick to aim up and down while slipping to the left and right using the left control stick. Since the boats are moving, aim in front of them and let loose with volleys of rockets. Don't worry about running out or waiting for the launchers to cool down. You can fire these rockets all the live long day. After both boats slip beneath the surface of the river, keep following the river as it makes a turn to the right.

Collectibles in this area: 0
Gold in this area: 0

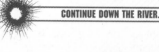

Fire rockets at the enemy boats.

If you take damage from the boats, land near this house to make repairs before continuing on.

★ DESTROY MILITARY INFRASTRUCTURE ★

DISTRACT AND CRIPPLE THE SERDARISTAN ARMY BY DESTROYING VITAL MATERIALS AND SUPPLIES.

> DESTROY THE FUEL SILOS   > DESTROY THE MILITARY BARRACKS   > DESTROY THE RADIO EQUIPMENT

Collectibles in this area: 0
Gold in this area: 2

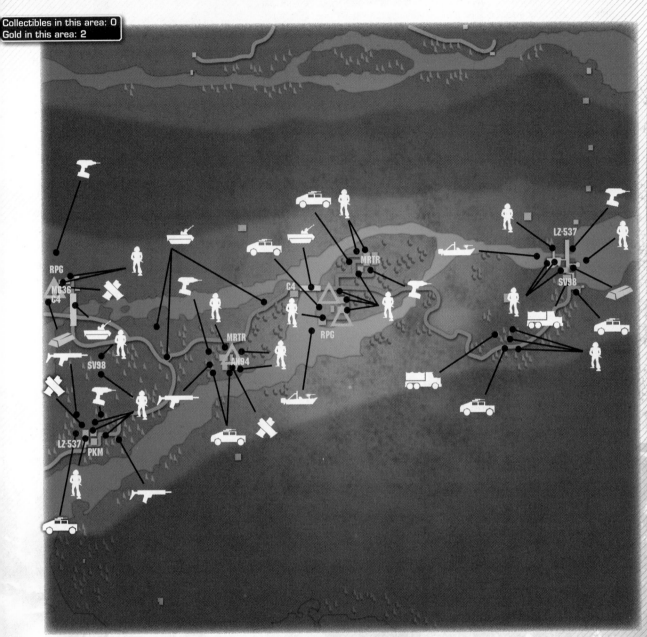

Enemies are defending the dam up ahead.

After following the river around the bend, you find yourself flying west. Up ahead in the distance you can see a dam across the river. While you have engaged some boats and trucks, this is the part of the mission where you really begin to run into enemy resistance. The ex-president informs you that most of Serdaristan's military is in this river valley. If you want to have a chance of getting out, you need to create a diversion. Destroying the enemy's military infrastructure will divert their attention away from a single helicopter trying to escape.

Welcome · Basic Training · Infantry · Vehicles · Campaign · Multiplayer · Appendix

Welcome to Bad Company | Acta non Verba | Crossing Over | Par for the Course | **Air Force One** | Crash and Grab | Ghost Town

NOTE ★★

This part of the mission can be completed as quickly or slowly as desired. With a helicopter, you can quickly move about the battlefield to attack targets and then get away before the enemy can regroup to counterattack. However, if you want to explore this area and pick up some weapons and equipment, you need to take your time and put your feet on the ground a lot.

Hammer the dam with rockets.

The dam represents the entrance to enemy territory. It is defended by infantry, some of whom are armed with RPGs, so use caution when engaging them. As you approach, begin firing rockets from a distance to try to kill as many enemies as you can before they start returning fire. Use the rockets while Haggard goes after enemies with the cannon. Be sure to hit the structures on the south end hard since there are some soldiers hiding in them. Then eliminate any other soldiers out on the dam itself.

Land at the north end of the dam.

Once the area around the dam is clear, land in the open spot just north of the dam. There are some things to pick up before continuing on. First off, repair the helicopter if you sustained any damage during the fight at the dam. Then check out the nearby shed to find a laser designator. That can come in handy later on, so pick it up. Plus it leaves the power tool near a landing spot in case you need to return for repairs later.

Watch out for surviving enemies as you walk across the dam.

Don't forget to steal a gold bar while you are here.

Make your way south across the dam. Since there could still be enemies alive in the area and hiding to ambush you, use caution and continue to the concrete building. Inside is an SV98 sniper rifle. In addition, another room contains some mercenary gold. Steal the bar from the case and then exit the building. Once you have picked up everything you want, head back to the helicopter and take off.

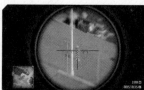

On the west side of the dam, way down at the bottom, the enemy has a small base. Use the sniper rifle while positioned on a ledge near the top of the dam to neutralize all of the enemies down below.

DESTROY THE FUEL SILOS

The fuel silos, and lots of enemies, are on this first island.

As you fly west from the dam, you see an island in the middle of the river. This is where the three groups of fuel silos are located. From the air, you can quickly destroy all three sets of targets with long range rocket fire. The silos are large and you really only need one hit on each group to destroy them all. As long as you stay moving, you don't really have to worry about the infantry on this island. However, as you near the middle of the island, an AAV rolls out on to the bridge to try to shoot you down. The AAV is essentially an IFV body with an anti-aircraft gun on top instead of a turret. Since it is on the bridge, fire volleys of rockets at the bridge and vehicle. If you don't hit and destroy the vehicle with rockets, you will at least destroy the bridge beneath the AAV and it will fall into the river and be destroyed. If you feel the need to do a little shoplifting, land on this island

One rocket hit on a fuel silo blows it up as well as the adjacent silos.

to pick up a power tool, a mortar strike designator, and an RPG. However, you need to clear out an area of enemies before landing the chopper.

Fire on the AAV from a distance to avoid getting hit by its fire.

FIGHTING ON LAND

In addition to completing the three main objectives for this part of the mission by using the helicopter, you can also achieve the same results with good old ground combat. Unless you destroyed it during the bombardment of the dam, you can climb into an armored jeep and follow the road from the dam down to the west. Haggard comes with you while Sarge and Sweetwater stay behind with the helicopter. While on the ground, you have to clear out a lot of enemy soldiers who are just waiting to try and kill you. Be sure to use a lot of the gadgets such as the mortar strike designator or the laser designator.

The enemy sets up a roadblock to the west of the dam. Use the vehicle's machine gun to destroy the opposition.

 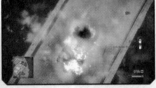

Use the laser designator to drop a guided bomb on top of the AAVs in this area.

FIGHTING ON THE WATER

Another way to complete these objectives is by stealing an enemy boat and using it to spread terror down the river. The patrol boats have two grenade launchers which will take care of fuel silos as well as barracks. Two of the groups of fuel silos are near the water as is the military barracks. You may have to park the boat and destroy the third group of fuel silos on foot since it is not close enough to the water to use the boat's grenade launcher.

Clear out the enemies at this small base at the bottom of the dam, then land the helicopter to go for a boat ride.

You can even use the boat to destroy the AAV. Just blow up the bridge underneath it.

DESTROY THE MILITARY BARRACKS

The next targets are the military barracks located on the second island. Stay right over the river to the south of this island, then fire volleys of grenades at the blue barracks to destroy this objective. Again,

Rockets make short work of the barracks.

by staying at a distance, you can avoid a lot of enemy fire. Within the burned out barracks, you can pick up a mortar strike designator, an AN94 assault rifle, and a power tool.

DESTROY THE RADIO EQUIPMENT

The last objective in this area is the radio equipment. To get to it, follow the river around the second island. You have to engage at least one AAV along the way as well as another on the bridge leading to the radio base.

Destroy the AAV on the tall bridge leading to the radio equipment.

As before, target the bridge and watch the AAV fall into the river a long way below.

Welcome · Basic Training · Infantry · Vehicles · Campaign · Multiplayer · Appendix

Welcome to Bad Company | Acta non Verba | Crossing Over | Par for the Course | Air Force One | Crash and Grab | Ghost Town

Hit all of the structures in the radio base to clear it out, then land your helicopter.

The radio equipment to destroy is in the basement of the large concrete building. In order to get to it, you must land the helicopter. Luckily, a landing pad is provided in the northern corner of the base. Fire volleys of rockets at all the buildings to blow out their walls so no enemies are hiding. Then, touch down and disembark from the helicopter along with Haggard.

Watch out for an enemy armored jeep as you move toward the objective.

Upon landing, hop out of the helicopter and make sure the area is secure by looking for muzzle flashes from enemy weapons. After it is safe, repair any damage the helicopter may have

Clear out the concrete building where the radio equipment is located.

sustained. You will not have time to fix it on your way out of here. If needed, pick up a power tool to the north of the landing pad. Now head south toward the two-story concrete building where your objective is waiting. An armored jeep may approach form the west, so stay alert. If you don't have an RPG to shoot at it, fire at the gunner, then at the infantry around it. Once the threat has been eliminated, continue to the building. Since this is an enemy headquarters, expect some soldiers to be waiting for you. Clear out the first floor, then head down the stairs to the basement level.

There is a gold bar waiting downstairs.

Clear out the soldiers guarding the radio equipment, then place C4 on it.

When you get to the bottom of the stairs, turn to your left and enter a side room. Inside is a mercenary case. Open it to steal a gold bar. Also stop by the ammo box to fill up your supply. There is also some C4 in this area. Pick it up. Walk past the stairway and approach a doorway on the right. The radio equipment is inside the next room—as well as lots of soldiers. If you have a hand grenade, lob one into the room to kill or at least flush out some enemies. Get ready to start firing as they come pouring out of the room. If necessary, backtrack to the room where you found the gold and use the walls to the side of the doorway for cover. Neutralize all of the threats in the basement, then move into the control room and place two explosive charges on the radio—one on each side. Exit the room and blow the charges to complete the objective.

Another armored jeep is waiting outside.

Get the chopper up in the air and ready to fight.

As you exit the building, get ready for another fight. Even though you cleared out this base previously, reinforcements have arrived, including an armored jeep. Rather than stopping to fight, run for the helicopter. Take off and switch to targeting view while you turn to face the enemy vehicle. Let loose with volleys of rockets as you strafe to the left to get a better field of fire while making it more difficult for the enemy to hit your moving aircraft. Once the vehicle has been destroyed, either stay to mop up the infantry or just fly away. If you clear out the soldiers, land the helicopter to repair any damage before continuing on.

If you are looking for some weapons or equipment, there are a couple places to explore to the south of the base with the radio equipment. The house just south of the bridge contains several soldiers as well as an SV98 sniper rifle. An enemy base even farther south on that same island has even more soldiers as well as a power tool, PKM light machine gun, and a LZ-537 laser designator.

★ MOVE OUT ★

KEEP ON FLYING DOWN THE RIVER.

▸ FOLLOW THE RIVER

Collectibles in this area: 0
Gold in this area: 1

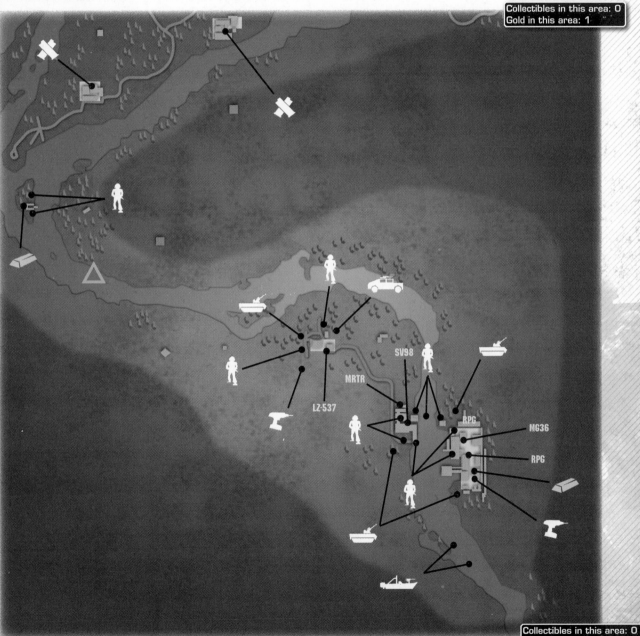

SV98

MRTR

LZ-537

RPG

MG36

RPG

Collectibles in this area: 0
Gold in this area: 1

PRIMA Official Game Guide

BATTLEFIELD BAD COMPANY

Welcome · Basic Training · Infantry · Vehicles · Campaign · Multiplayer · Appendix

Welcome to Bad Company | Acta non Verba | Crossing Over | Par for the Course | **Air Force One** | Crash and Grab | Ghost Town

FOLLOW THE RIVER

Fly south to follow the river.

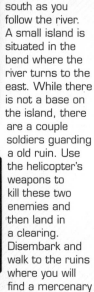

Fly the helicopter south as you follow the river. A small island is situated in the bend where the river turns to the east. While there is not a base on the island, there are a couple soldiers guarding a old ruin. Use the helicopter's weapons to kill these two enemies and then land in a clearing. Disembark and walk to the ruins where you will find a mercenary case.

Kill the two soldiers near the ruins on the small island.

The soldiers were guarding a gold bar. Since they won't be needing it, take it, then head back to the helicopter. Take off and continue following the river to the east.

Steal some more gold from the mercenaries.

★ CUT OFF SERDAR'S SUPPLY LINES ★

 **DESTROY THE TRUCKS**    **DESTROY THE INCOMING BOATS**

> MAKE SURE THAT NO ENEMY SUPPLY TRUCKS SURVIVE.

DESTROY THE TRUCKS

Rocket the AAV before it rocks you.

Your new orders are to destroy the enemy trucks around a port facility. However, up ahead are a few underground missile silos. While they do not threaten

Land by the large missile silo.

you, the AAV guarding them is a problem. Watch for the red targeting icon to appear, then get ready to fire volleys of rockets at the vehicle. If it starts firing, slip or strafe to one side while keeping your nose pointed at the AAV. After it is a smoking wreck, move in and clear out any infantry nearby so

you can land the helicopter without coming under immediate attack. If you don't already have one, pick up a LZ-537 laser designator. This will come in handy.

Drive the armored jeep toward the port.

Commandeer the armored jeep parked near the building and follow the road leading to the port. Before you get to the port, turn off the road and head up the hill to the right. Halt before you get to the top and dismount. Continue the rest of the way on foot. The hill provides a great vantage point for calling in air strikes with your laser designator. The port is defended by three AAVs. One is located at the south end of the western docks while two more are on the eastern docks—at the north and south ends, respectively. Crouch down so you are harder to see, and then use the laser designator to target the western AAV first, since it is the biggest threat to you on foot. After you get a lock, steer the bomb right onto the top of the AAV. Even a near miss destroys the vehicle. Repeat the process for the southeastern AAV as well. The northeastern AAV can be difficult to see. However, take aim at one of the trucks in the northeast and when you get control of the bomb, steer it to the left to try and find the AAV. If nothing else, you will probably destroy some trees between you and the target, giving a better line of sight so you can then laser the target and guide a bomb onto the final air defense at the port.

Fly the helicopter toward the port.

Now that the AAVs have been eliminated, walk back to the armored jeep and drive it back to the waiting helicopter. Climb aboard and take off. Fly along the road and begin attacking the enemies  on the western dock. Focus on the soldiers with RPGs first, killing them with volleys of rockets while Haggard fires the chin cannon. After this side is clear, you can land and look around the area for a mortar strike designator as well as a sniper rifle.

Fire rockets at the enemies along the western dock while Haggard uses the cannon to further the devastation.

★ TIP ★

Pick up the mortar strike designator and take it with you. It can come in handy during the last part of this mission.

DESTROY THE INCOMING BOATS

Two large patrol boats arrive on the scene after you start blowing up trucks.

After getting what you need on the west side of port, climb back into the helicopter and begin wreaking havoc on the east side. As soon as you destroy some of the trucks on this side, a couple of patrol boats come in from the south. Turn to face the new threats and launch volleys of rockets at them. Strafe right and left so you are a harder target for the enemy to hit. Score several hits on each boat to send them to the bottom of the river so you can continue your attack on the supply trucks.

★ TIP ★

You can eliminate most of the supply trucks while standing on the hilltop and calling in air strikes. After the AAVs are destroyed, start blowing up trucks. When the patrol boats arrive, target them as well. One direct hit with a bomb sinks these boats.

CAUTION ★★★

Don't destroy all of the supply trucks until you are ready to get your new orders. If you want to do some exploring, save at least one truck or you will miss your chance to pick up some goodies.

Land at the helipad.

Enter this building to find another gold bar.

A helipad is located in the northeastern part of the port. Clear out the surrounding area with your helicopter weapons, then land at this spot. Disembark, then continue engaging enemy infantry with Haggard at your side. There are several items you can pick up on this side of the base, including an MG36, some RPGs, and a power tool. However, be sure to check out the concrete building in the southern part of the eastern docks. Inside you can steal one more gold bar from the mercenaries. After you have taken what you want, head back to the helicopter. Be sure to repair it if needed. Then take off and destroy any remaining supply trucks.

Welcome - Basic Training - Infantry - Vehicles - Campaign - Multiplayer - Appendix

Welcome to Bad Company | Acta non Verba | Crossing Over | Par for the Course | **Air Force One** | Crash and Grab | Ghost Town

★ REACH THE REFUEL BASE ★

GET TO THE REFUEL BASE BEFORE YOU RUN OUT OF GAS.

▬ FOLLOW THE RIVER   ▬ LAND AT THE HELIPAD

Collectibles in this area: 0
Gold in this area: 0

FOLLOW THE RIVER

Keep following the river around a bend to the left.

Sink two more boats.

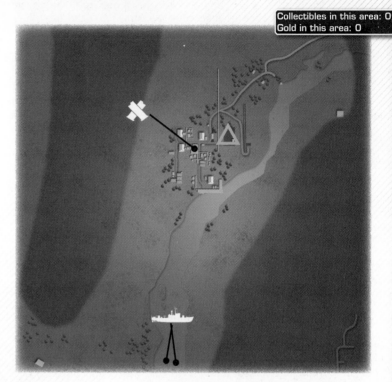

After destroying the last supply truck, the fuel alert begins flashing. Your helicopter is at bingo fuel which means you have just enough to get to the refuel base. Head south down the river and follow it around to the left as it makes a bend to the north. Just past the turn, you come across a couple enemy patrol boats. Armed with grenade launchers, they could damage your helicopter, so sink them with volleys of rockets. Keep moving while you attack since you don't have a lot of fuel to spare for this engagement.

LAND AT THE HELIPAD

Your new orders are to land at the helipad. As you fly past the rest of the base, fire rockets to cause some damage during your approach. However, don't stop to attack the base. Keep flying to make it to the helipad and land.

Touch down at the helipad at the northeastern corner of the base.

★ 96 ★

FIND A FUEL TRUCK AND BRING IT BACK TO THE HELICOPTER IN ORDER TO REFUEL.

▸ **FIND A FUEL TRUCK AND RETURN** ▸ **PROTECT THE HELICOPTER** ▸ **ESCAPE IN THE HELICOPTER**

Collectibles in this area: 0
Gold in this area: 1

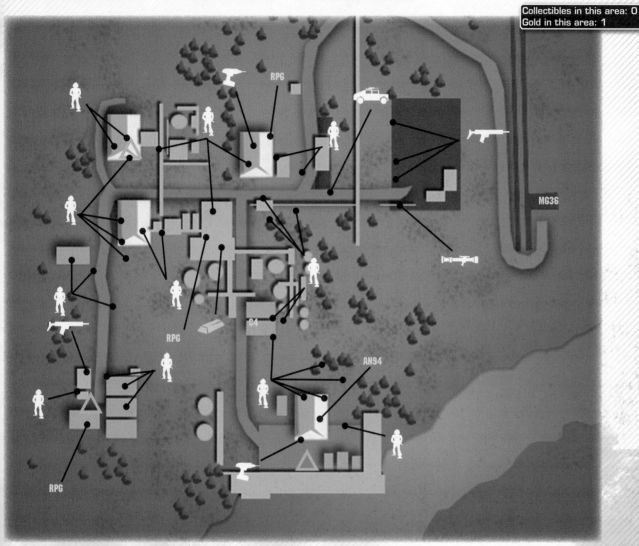

FIND A FUEL TRUCK AND RETURN

Man the defenses and fight off the enemy attack!

As soon as you land the helicopter, the soldiers at the base get ready to attack your position. Luckily, the helipad area has three machine guns and a rocket launcher to use for defense. In addition to lots of infantry, an armored jeep is also firing on your squad. While the rocket launcher is great for destroying the enemy vehicle, it is of little use against the soldiers. Therefore, man a machine gun. Fire on the armored jeep first, then work over the soldiers assaulting your position. Keep track of your health. If it gets low, let go of the machine gun, crouch, heal yourself, and then man the gun again. After

you fight off the attack, take a quick breath, then begin going after a fuel truck.

TIP

If you brought along the mortar strike designator, use it to call in artillery strikes on enemy troops as well as buildings. Not only can this reduce the number of soldiers you have to engage, it also blows out the walls of buildings, making it easier to detect enemies inside.

Enter this building west of the helipad area to find the last gold bar in this mission.

PRIMA Official Game Guide

BATTLEFIELD **BAD COMPANY**

Welcome · Basic Training · Infantry · Vehicles · Campaign · Multiplayer · Appendix

Welcome to Bad Company | Acta non Verba | Crossing Over | Par for the Course | **Air Force One** | Crash and Grab | Ghost Town

There are three fuel trucks on this base. Any one of them works for refueling the helicopter. The easiest one to get is the northern truck parked in a garage to the west of your position. The other two are in the south. However, not only do you have to fight more enemies to get to them, you also have to drive farther under enemy fire. Therefore, follow the road west. Move from cover to cover, neutralizing enemies as you find them. Use grenades, rockets, or even mortar strikes to punch holes in the buildings along the way to make sure they are clear. You want to secure both sides of the road since you will be driving a truck carrying flammable fuel. Be sure to explore the building on the south side of the road just past the guard tower. Inside find another mercenary case. Open it and steal a gold bar for your squad.

Clear out this building, then get into this fuel truck.

This soldier is waiting to the south of the garage to ambush you as you try to drive the truck back to the helipad.

Continue on to the garage where the truck is waiting. Be sure to check the building and the surrounding area to make sure you have eliminated all immediate threats. Then climb into the truck and start to drive out. However, quickly stop and jump out of the truck. As soon as you were ready to drive, a soldier just to the east of the garage comes out to attack. Kill him, then get back into the truck. Drive along the road as fast as you can since other enemies come after you to try to prevent your escape.

Put the pedal to the metal while driving along this straight shot to the helipad.

PROTECT THE HELICOPTER

The enemy is attacking again!

As soon as you get the truck to the helipad, Haggard starts refueling the helicopter. However, the enemy is not going to let you escape without a fight. They are headed your way. Not only do you have to stay alive, you also have to keep the soldiers away from the helicopter since they will attack it as well as your squad. If the helicopter is destroyed, there is no escape. Rush to the rocket launcher and take cover behind the sandbags. Fire your rifle or light machine gun at approaching soldiers. An armored jeep joins in the attack. As soon as you see it, get on the rocket launcher and eliminate the vehicle with a single hit. At this point, move north to one of the machine guns closer to the helicopter and mow down approaching enemies. Keep up the pressure until Haggard gets the refueling process completed.

As soon as you see the armored jeep, man the rocket launcher and destroy the enemy vehicle.

ESCAPE IN THE HELICOPTER

Armor is headed this way! Run for the helicopter!

As it seems like you have defeated the enemy attack, Haggard lets you know the chopper is fueled and ready to go. He finished not a moment too soon. The enemy has brought up some armor and it is headed down the road toward the helipad. Don't even think about trying to destroy it. Instead, run for the helicopter and climb in to make your escape.

Take off and escape from the base.

However, the enemy has sent their own aircraft after you. It doesn't look good.

CRASH AND GRAB

Collectibles in this mission: 2
Gold in this mission: 5

As I was piloting the helicopter with my squad aboard to escape from Serdaristan, another helicopter—this one a high-tech attack chopper—shot us down. That is the last thing I remember. When I came to, I was all alone. The wrecked helicopter was nearby as was a small village. While I was probably somewhere in Russia, I had no idea where, or even if the members of my squad were still alive. Luckily, I could get through to Miss July, our Army contact. The military had written off Bad Company as AWOL and dead. There would be no help coming. However, Miss July promised to feed information to me as she could. Other than that, I was on my own.

★ LOCATE SQUAD INSIDE THE VILLAGE ★

SEARCH THE NEARBY VILLAGE FOR YOUR SQUAD MATES.

▸ INVESTIGATE THE COMMAND POST

INVESTIGATE THE COMMAND POST

Collectibles in this area: 1
Gold in this area: 0

Your main weapon to begin with is a pistol.

In addition to grenades, you also carry three motion sensors.

PRIMA Official Game Guide

BATTLEFIELD
BAD COMPANY

Welcome · Basic Training · Infantry · Vehicles · Campaign · Multiplayer · Appendix

Welcome to Bad Company | Acta non Verba | Crossing Over | Par for the Course | Air Force One | **Crash and Grab** | Ghost Town

As soon as the mission starts, crouch down and take inventory. A convoy of trucks drives down the road, so you want to stay put for a bit anyway. A pistol is your only firearm. In addition to this, you have some hand grenades, an auto injector, and some motion sensors. The motion sensors can be thrown like a grenade and will show enemies that it detects on your minimap. These gadgets only work for a short amount of time. However, if thrown into a position in which you will be advancing, it can reveal enemies waiting to ambush you.

Take cover in a house.

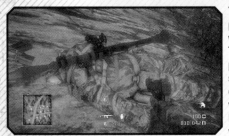

Kill one of the patrolling enemies and pick up his weapons.

Your initial position is to the west of a village. The command post is in the southeastern corner of the village. However, before you can worry about getting there, you have to get across the main road. A couple soldiers patrol the road individually. Since they are armed with assault rifles or shotguns, they have an advantage over you and your pistol. However, you have surprise on your side. Crouch down and move to the house to the south where your helicopter crashed. Take cover inside this building and wait for the enemy to appear. Use ironsights to increase your accuracy and let loose with four or five shots to make sure you drop the soldier. Since your gunfire may have alerted other nearby soldiers, quickly reload so you have a full clip in your pistol and take a brief look around. If no one comes right away, run over to the body of the soldier you killed and pick up his weapon. Take whatever it is. You can always swap again later. Assault rifles or light machine guns are the best choices. Due to the fact that captured weapons are usually low on ammo, be sure to check other enemies you neutralize and pick up their ammo by walking over their dropped weapons.

Watch for enemies to come out of the houses to attack.

While the desire for cover might make you think the best tactic is to move through the village, going from house to house and clearing as you go, that is not a good idea—especially since you are alone.

Approach the command center from the south.

Though you do get some cover, the enemy will surround you. Instead, stay to the perimeter of the village and use trees and rocks for cover. You'll also face a lot less enemies on the perimeter. The main threat comes from the soldiers patrolling to the east and south of the village as well as a couple enemies who hide in the house to the northwest of the command center. Launch or throw grenades to flush them out so they don't ambush you later.

Clear the immediate area, then enter the command center.

After killing the soldiers right around the command center, move into the building to see if you can find your squad. They are not there, however. Miss July suggests trying the communications center to the east. Once MJ signs off, quickly pick up the M136 rocket launcher located in the command center to unlock a collectible. Keep your assault rifle or light machine gun for now, however.

Pick up the rocket launcher.

The soldiers come from the north and west. They will try to flank you, so pull back to the southern side of the command center if necessary to

find cover after explosions take out the northern walls.

Enemy troops learned you are in the command center and move to kill you. An armored jeep arrives shortly after you talk to Miss July. Destroy the vehicle with a single rocket hit from your launcher, then start mowing down infantry as they advance on your position. Try to use cover, but watch out for explosive crates and barrels. If you are close by when they blow, you receive some serious hurt. Stay around the command center until you have cleared all nearby enemies.

Another option for getting to the command center is to advance from the north. Move to the house north of your starting position at the beginning of the mission. Clear out the soldiers patrolling north of the village, then move in from the east. This allows you to approach a grenade launcher from behind and kill the soldier manning it. Take control of the grenade launcher and start blowing holes in the walls of nearby houses in case enemies are hiding in them. Near the grenade launcher, you can also find an ammo crate to fully restock your captured weapons.

★ LEARN THE LOCATION OF THE SQUAD ★

FIND OUT WHERE YOUR SQUAD MATES ARE HELD. SEARCH THE COMMUNICATION CENTER FOR CLUES.

▸ REACH THE COMMUNICATIONS CENTER   ▸ INVESTIGATE THE SECURITY ROOM

MAP ON NEXT PAGE

Pick up the M95 sniper rifle. It is a collectible you want to keep for now.

Clear the far bank of the river by using the sniper rifle.

A boat is waiting for you at the dock.

It's time to leave the command center. However, before you do, pick up the M95 sniper rifle in the building. This is one collectible you want to keep—at least for now. Advance down to the river where a boat is waiting for you. However, before you get in, it is a good idea to do some sniping. A house is located across the river. There are three soldiers patrolling around that area. Since one of them is armed with an RPG, they are a major threat to you. Locate all three first, then start shooting them. The M95 is a powerful sniper rifle, so one hit does the job. Also, look down the river to the southwest to see if you can detect soldiers patrolling the bridge. They are armed with RPGs. Try to shoot them now so you can drive right under the bridge without any problems.

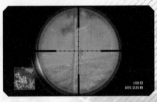

An armored jeep is parked near a couple more boats at the northern dock. You can take to the roads instead of the river if you want.

However, you have to travel farther and face more resistance when traveling by ground. In addition, most enemy defenses, such as machine guns, are positioned to cover the roads.

PRIMA Official Game Guide

BATTLEFIELD BAD COMPANY

Welcome · Basic Training · Infantry · Vehicles · Campaign · Multiplayer · Appendix

Welcome to Bad Company | Acta non Verba | Crossing Over | Par for the Course | Air Force One | **Crash and Grab** | Ghost Town

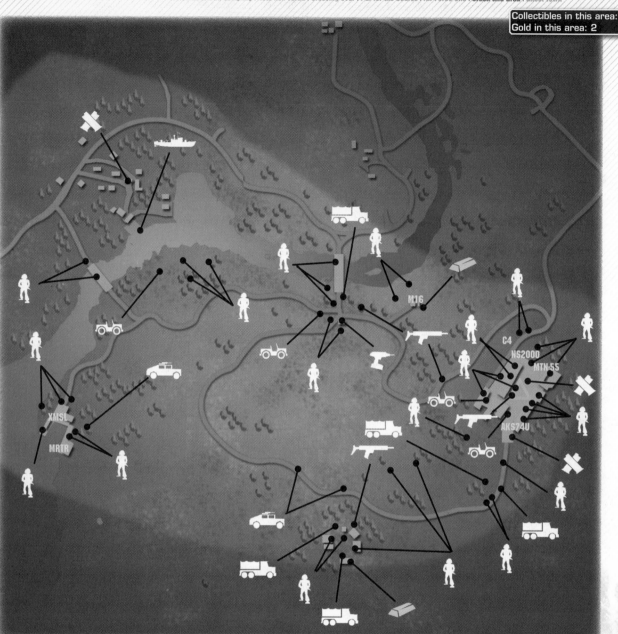

Collectibles in this area: 1
Gold in this area: 2

XMSL
MRTR
M16
C4
NS2000
MTN-55
AKS74U

REACH THE COMMUNICATIONS CENTER

Follow the river as it flows to the southwest.

In order to get to the docks in the southwest, you have to drive your boat under a bridge. A couple soldiers with RPGs are waiting. A few hits will sink your boat and leave you dead in the water—literally.

Use the grenade launchers to blow up the bridge where soldiers are waiting to ambush you with RPGs.

Therefore, as you get closer to the bridge and can see the enemy, press the switch seats button once to take control of the forward grenade launcher. Fire at the sides of the bridge where the enemies are hiding. When the grenade launcher stops to cool down and reload, press the switch seats button twice to return to the driver's seat. Gun the engines to get under the bridge and continue on at full speed, in case some of the enemies survived.

Land on the southeastern part of the dock.

Drive the armored jeep north along the road.

Clear out enemies in the eastern part of the dock area first.

Keep the boat at full speed all the way to the docks. Park the boat near the southeastern docks and get out. There are a couple soldiers patrolling the eastern part of this area. Kill both of them, then move into the house on this side to find a mortar strike designator. Pick it up, and then call in an artillery strike on the western part of the docks to get rid of the enemy soldiers there. Keep an eye on the minimap to you can see if you hit the enemies or need to call in another strike.

Trade it in for a new ride.

The armored jeep is already on a trail leading to the east. However, turn it around and take the main road leading north out of the dock area. This takes you past the bridge you drove the boat under, so watch out for soldiers with RPGs that might have survived your maritime attack. Just past the bridge, turn off the road to approach a house near the river. There were three soldiers patrolling this area, but you should have shot them all with the sniper rifle before taking the boat for a downriver excursion. If that is the case, the next task is easy. A jeep is parked next to the house. Climb out of the armored jeep and get into the smaller jeep. While you give up some of the protection of the larger vehicle, the smaller jeep is armed not only with a machine gun, but also a grenade launcher. The greater firepower comes in handy as you look for your missing squad mates.

The mortar strike designator can come in handy during several parts of this mission. Remember to use this gadget. Whenever a defensive position is in your way, find a safe spot with a view of the target, then call in the mortars. This tactic can also be used to destroy vehicles. Armored vehicles may require a couple bombardments before they are neutralized.

Take the jeep for a spin.

Drive the jeep onto the road, then follow the road to the east. As you approach a crossroads near another bridge, halt and dismount from the jeep. It is easier to clear out this crossroads on foot. Crouch down and move through the trees and cover to the right side of the road as you approach the enemy. In addition to a machine gun, there is also a number of soldiers. Once you see the enemy machine gun, find a good spot with cover, then start the engagement by shooting the soldier manning the machine gun. As soon as you open fire, the action goes into overdrive as all of the soldiers in the area start trying to kill you. Keep an eye on the minimap to see where they are because the trees that provide you cover also limit your vision.

Clear out the crossroads on foot.

Clear out the northern houses and pick up an XM8 LMG

All that remains are the two soldiers in the buildings to the north of the docks. You can once again call in a mortar strike on the enemy to blow them away, then go pick up the collectible in one of the houses—an XM8 light machine gun. Pick up and keep this collectible since it is more useful now than a sniper rifle. By now, the docks should be clear, so hop into the armored jeep parked here and roll up your sleeves for some more work.

PRIMA Official Game Guide

BAD COMPANY
BATTLEFIELD

Welcome · Basic Training · Infantry · Vehicles · Campaign · Multiplayer · Appendix

Welcome to Bad Company | Acta non Verba | Crossing Over | Par for the Course | Air Force One | **Crash and Grab** | Ghost Town

If necessary, pull back to the jeep to use its weapons for additional firepower. As you clear the area right around the intersection, also look to the north for soldiers out on the bridge. Kill them as well, so they don't sneak up behind you. The only item here is a power tool. Repair your jeep if needed. There is also another jeep parked along the road which you can borrow. Just make sure you leave with your mortar strike designator instead of the power tool.

Fire the jeep's grenade launcher at the house to clear out any enemies waiting inside.

Another gold bar waits for you.

Now that the crossroads is clear, get into a jeep and continue east down the road. Turn at the next left, which is not too far away. The road ends at a house where a couple of soldiers are guarding something you want. As you approach the house, press the switch seat button once to take control of the grenade launcher. Begin firing at the house to blow holes in the wall, and kill the soldiers inside—or wherever they may be in this area. Once they are dead, get out of the jeep and move into the house to pick up an M16 assault rifle. While the XM8 light machine gun is a good weapon, the assault rifle gives you the grenade launcher as well. Depending on your style of play, use the best weapon for you. Before you leave, look around the outside of the house to find a mercenary case. Open it and take the gold bar to share with your squad—once you find them.

Assaulting the communications center from the front can be tough since most of its defenses are covering that entrance.

Continuing east down the road will take you right to the communications center. Even though that is where you want to go, the enemy will be expecting you to come at them through their main entrance, and they have lots of defenses waiting for you. If you want to try it anyway, go ahead. The enemy has a machine gun positioned along the side of the road before you even get to the base. Then, once you reach the main gate, be ready for several soldiers there as well as more inside. Don't try to race into the base, crashing through the gate at full speed and running over anyone who gets in your way. This tactic keeps enemies behind you and, before you know it, you will be shot at from all sides. Instead, methodically make your way to the entrance, killing all of the soldiers near the gate with grenades and machine gun fire from the jeep. Then drive through the gate and be ready to switch to the gunner's seat as soon as you see enemies.

Don't you have a mortar strike designator in your pocket? Why not use it to blow away the front gate—guards included—and then continue to call in artillery strikes against machine gun positions and other defenses.

A couple of armored jeeps patrol the southern road. Blast them.

Kill the soldier manning the machine gun in the tower.

It is much easier to assault the communications center from the back door. Instead of driving east down the road, go west. Take a left at the crossroads and follow this road south, then around to the east. Along the way, you run into a couple of armored jeeps. Use your jeep's weapons to destroy the first one. If your jeep is taking damage, dismount and aim at the soldier manning the machine gun on the second armored jeep. Kill him and the rest of the soldiers around the enemy vehicle, but try to leave the armored jeep as undamaged as possible. This way, if your jeep is about to blow up, you have another vehicle to use. Just past where you run into those enemies, turn right off the road to approach a small base. It is guarded by a machine gun in a tower with more soldiers patrolling around as well. Use your vehicle's weapon to kill the guard in the tower, then finish off the remaining soldiers. Once the base is clear, enter the building with the mercenary sign outside to find a gold bar.

The mercenary sign shows where to find gold in this base.

Get back to your vehicle and continue driving east down the road. Near where the road turns to the north, a couple of trucks block your path. Kill the enemy soldiers at this roadblock, then move out on foot. There are enemy snipers to the north of the road. Rush to cover, then crouch down. By the roadblock, head north up a hill to kill a sniper who overlooks the communications center below. Then take his rifle temporarily so you can snipe at enemies in the base to the north. From this position, you can also call in mortar attacks. Clear out as many enemies as you can, then pick up your other weapon and head into the base.

A great spot for sniping.

INVESTIGATE THE SECURITY ROOM

Clear out the outside of the main building.

Enter the base and get ready for some fighting. There are some jeeps parked in the base that you can use as weapons platforms to help you clear out all enemies around the outside of the main building. Use the grenade launchers to blow holes in the wall to make it easier to clear enemies out. Work your way around the outside of the main building, clearing as you go. Some enemies like to hide up high on catwalks. Shoot them or they will try to kill you when you move past them. There are also several weapons and gadgets you can pick up around the base.

Watch out for enemies up high.

Enter the building and head down these stairs to get to the security room.

Once the area outside the main building is clear, it is time to go inside. Move in cautiously, watching for an ambush, then head down the stairs to get to the security room. Kill any soldiers along the way. Inside the security room, watch a video screen of the mercenary leader talking to your ex-president friend. You learn that your squad mates are being held in an old monastery. Now you know where you must go. Get out of the communications center and back on the road.

RESCUE THE SQUAD

LIBERATE THE SQUAD FROM THE OLD MONASTERY.

▸ REACH THE MONASTERY　　▸ LOCATE THE SQUAD

MAP ON NEXT PAGE

Engage the enemies surrounding you as you exit the main building.

As you exit the main building, you discover that the base you previously secured is no longer clear. Enemy reinforcements have arrived and you must now fight for your life. Start firing away with your weapon. If you need more ammo, there is an ammo box inside the main building on the first floor. As usual, watch the minimap to see where the soldiers are moving to set up

shots before you see them visually. Make your way to one of the parked jeeps and get driving. Head down the ramp to the lower level and hang a right. Then gun it as you race to the main entrance of the communications center. Crash through the gate to make your escape.

Drive down the ramp, and then turn right to race out the main entrance.

PRIMA Official Game Guide

BAD COMPANY
BATTLEFIELD

Welcome ‧ Basic Training ‧ Infantry ‧ Vehicles ‧ Campaign ‧ Multiplayer ‧ Appendix

Welcome to Bad Company | Acta non Verba | Crossing Over | Par for the Course | Air Force One | **Crash and Grab** | Ghost Town

REACH THE MONASTERY

Blow up a couple enemy jeeps as you drive along the road.

After exiting the communications center base, keep driving north toward a small collection of homes, which is one of your way points to the monastery. However, before you get there, a couple of enemy-driven jeeps come at you on the road. Quickly switch seats to the grenade launcher and fire away. If the grenade launcher overheats, switch to the machine gun and keep firing until both enemy jeeps are destroyed.

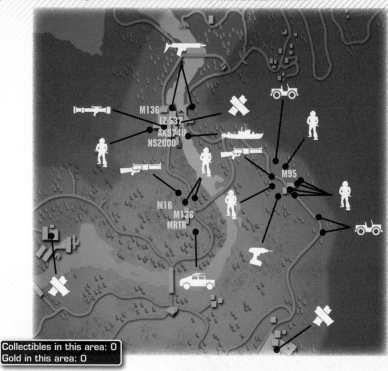

Collectibles in this area: 0
Gold in this area: 0

Stay back and let the mortars start clearing the town for you.

Drive across this ford and then use the jeep's grenade launcher to attack the enemies in this small settlement.

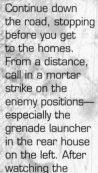

Continue down the road, stopping before you get to the homes. From a distance, call in a mortar strike on the enemy positions—especially the grenade launcher in the rear house on the left. After watching the

Then move in and finish off any survivors.

destruction rain down on the enemy a couple times, move in and finish off any remaining soldiers. You can find a power tool to repair your jeep if necessary as well as a M95 sniper rifle. There is also another jeep on the far side of this area which you can take if the previous one is in poor shape.

Get back into a vehicle and follow the road to the northwest. When you come to a fork in the road, turn left and head south. You have to cross the river at a shallow ford. However, as you drive up the opposite bank, get ready for a fight. The enemy have taken over the buildings and are waiting for you with a grenade launcher as well as an armored jeep. Use your jeep's grenade launcher to silence the enemy firepower. After it is all clear, pick up an M16 in one of the buildings. While there is a rocket launcher and mortar strike designator here as well, just keep your previous mortar strike designator.

Use the jeep's grenade launcher to clear out the next base.

TIP

The sniper rifle can be used in the next fight. Go ahead and grab it if you like sniping. You can then swap it out for an M16 in one of the buildings in that same area.

The next engagement is to the north. Drive your jeep down the road, but halt before you enter the base. Fire grenades at the enemies near the entrance, drive closer until you find more soldiers, and repeat the process. As in previous engagements, watch the minimap and clear out this base, including the machine guns, one of which is on a rooftop. While you can pick up some weapons, you might also consider the LZ-537. This laser designator allows you to call in air strikes against vehicles.

You also have to move in on foot to finish securing this area and to check out the goodies you can pick up.

Don't forget that the laser designator can only lock on to enemy vehicles. However, once the bomb is dropped, you can steer it to hit anything nearby, such as defensive positions.

Cross the river again at this ford.

Get back into a jeep. There are a few in the area if you need a new one. Follow the road north out of this base and cross the river at the ford where the road ends. After crossing the river, Miss July gives you some additional information and reveals more of the map to you.

Collectibles in this area: 0
Gold in this area: 3

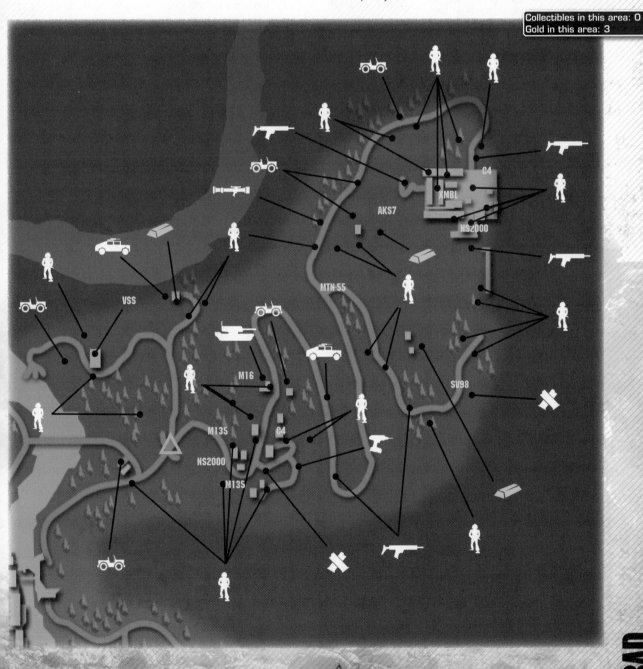

PRIMA Official Game Guide

BAD COMPANY
BATTLEFIELD

Welcome · Basic Training · Infantry · Vehicles · Campaign · Multiplayer · Appendix

Welcome to Bad Company | Acta non Verba | Crossing Over | Par for the Course | Air Force One | **Crash and Grab** | Ghost Town

A couple of enemies are in or around this house on the other side of the ford.

Clear out this house and the surrounding area as well.

As soon as you cross the river, get ready to engage a couple of soldiers. You shouldn't even have to leave your jeep—just use the grenade launcher to take them out. Instead of following the road toward your objective, turn north and drive cross country to another home. Clear it out of enemies as well. Inside, pick up a VSS sniper rifle. It comes in handy soon and you can always get another assault rifle later.

Drive east, kill a couple soldiers, and pick up a gold bar.

There is one more home just to the east. Follow the road there and kill the two soldiers patrolling this area. Once again, take care of this while staying on the jeep. In addition to an armored jeep here, there is also a mercenary case with a bar of gold. Get the gold and then head south toward the house near the ford.

A tank is hiding in the village. Try to spot it using a sniper rifle or ironsights before it sees you.

You need to clear out this village on foot if you want to explore for weapons and gadgets.

The monastery is at the top of the mountain overlooking this valley. The road leading up to the top passes through a large village. Since you have to get through the village, it is important to clear it out as much as possible. The main threat you can't avoid is a tank positioned near the northern part of the village. The first task is to locate the tank while staying at a distance. You can destroy the tank in a number of ways. If you have the laser designator, target the tank, then guide the bomb right on top of the vehicle to destroy it. You can also call in mortar strikes on the tank. It takes two strikes to kill the tank. After the tank is destroyed, drive into the village and begin engaging enemy soldiers. Dismount and continue on foot if you want to check out what this village has to offer. While there are a couple rocket launchers, stick with the mortar strike if you still have it.

Blow up this armored jeep.

Before leaving the village, make sure you have a fully repaired vehicle. There are jeeps here as well as a power tool to repair your current vehicle. Now follow the road that leads north out of the village.

Call in a mortar strike on the machine gun position.

After following the road around a turn that leads to the south, an armored jeep approaches. Quickly switch seats and fire grenades at the vehicle and dismounted infantry to clear the road. Drive a bit farther down the road, then stop before you get to the next turn. The enemy has positioned a machine gun there. Call in a mortar strike on that position to clear the road. Once the machine gun is eliminated, get back into your vehicle and follow the road around to the north once again.

Watch for a couple snipers to the northeast of the road.

Go back across the bridge to the barbed wire where you parked before assaulting the checkpoint. Drive around the barbed wire and follow a path to the southeast. At the turn, a machine gun waits to attack

Neutralize the enemies at the checkpoint by the bridge.

As you are driving, snipers up the hill from the road fire on you. It is a good idea to stop and take them out with your assault rifle. Heal yourself if needed, then continue on down the road. Stop by the barbed wire

that blocks a path off to the right. From that spot engage the enemy soldiers who are up ahead at a checkpoint by a bridge. Shoot them with your weapon or call in a mortar strike on them. Then move in and finish them off.

Kill the soldiers at the machine gun along the way.

you. Kill the soldiers there with your vehicle's weapon, then pick up a sniper rifle off of one of the dead soldiers. There are snipers around here, so take them out with your sniper rifle. Since you have limited ammo when taking a dead enemy's weapon, make your way north to the ammo box in some ruins. You can also find a fully loaded SV98 sniper rifle there.

Follow a path up the side of the mountain to this ruin where you can find some more gold.

After securing the checkpoint, cross over the bridge and look up to the east. The ruins about halfway up the mountain contain a case with a gold bar. To get there, walk to the east until you find a path that leads north up to the ruins. Get the gold, then head back down to your vehicle by the bridge. If you need another vehicle, there is a jeep parked off to the side of the road.

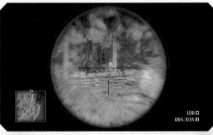

As you are walking toward the ammo box from the machine gun position, look off to your left for a trail with the mercenary sign. Follow this trail to some ruins where you find the last gold bar in this mission.

After picking up a sniper rifle and some gold, drive up the road to the end, killing enemies patrolling the road as you go. When you get to the foot bridge, get out and snipe the soldier on the far side next to

Use your sniper rifle to eliminate the soldier on the machine gun on the other side of the foot bridge.

the machine gun. Rush across the bridge to the other side and begin clearing out the barracks in this area. There are more soldiers near the main entrance to the north. Use your sniper rifle to neutralize those threats as well before entering the monastery itself.

This trail leads to the back door of the monastery.

Clear out the area in front of the monastery with your sniper rifle.

PRIMA Official Game Guide

BATTLEFIELD BAD COMPANY

Welcome · Basic Training · Infantry · Vehicles · Campaign · Multiplayer · Appendix

Welcome to Bad Company | Acta non Verba | Crossing Over | Par for the Course | Air Force One | **Crash and Grab** | Ghost Town

LOCATE THE SQUAD

It is now time to enter the monastery. Get a shotgun or assault rifle from one of the dead enemies or from inside the southern guard tower so you have a weapon better suited for close-quarters fighting. After

Since the sniper rifle is not good for close-up fighting, take along the NS2000 shotgun located in the southern guard tower.

entering the monastery, turn to the left, shooting enemies in the nearby barracks, then pick up the XM8 LMG sitting on a weapons case. This light machine gun makes clearing the monastery a lot easier. There is a machine gun at the western end of the monastery, so take cover from it, and kill the gunner as soon as you can. Use grenades and gunfire to clear out this entire area since you have to come out this way to make your escape in a bit.

Mow down enemies near the barracks as well as on the catwalk.

Once the courtyard is clear, move through the doorway behind the machine gun. Follow the hallway and kill the soldiers at the end to meet up with your squad mates.

★ REACH THE RIVER MOUTH ★

LOCATE FORMER PRESIDENT SERDAR AND FLEE RUSSIA.

LOCATE SERDAR

LOCATE SERDAR

Now that all of you are together, it is time to get out of here.

An enemy IFV is waiting on the other side of the bridge. Destroy it.

As you approach the bridge checkpoint, slow down. The enemy has positioned an IFV to stop you. Call in mortar or air strikes to get rid of it, depending on what you have. Another option is to use the rocket launcher on your side of the bridge. Once the enemy vehicle is destroyed, drive your own vehicle across the bridge and continue down the road.

Fight your way out of the monastery to the main entrance.

After getting the squad back together again, it is time to get out of Dodge. Move back to the courtyard and engage the enemy soldiers trying to come get you. Exit the courtyard, then shoot at the soldiers to the north blocking your way out. Your squad helps you out. Once the exit is clear, jump into a nearby jeep and race out past the enemy trucks and follow the road down the mountain.

A roadblock is set up at the next bridge.

Halt your vehicle before you get to the turn to the right at the end of the road. Dismount and look down the hill to see some trucks and soldiers setting up a roadblock. Don't try to crash through this, because the soldiers have RPGs. Instead, try to kill the enemy from your position. Then you can drive through the roadblock without taking any fire. Now drive all the way to the village, running over any soldiers who are foolish enough to stand out in the middle of the road to shoot at you.

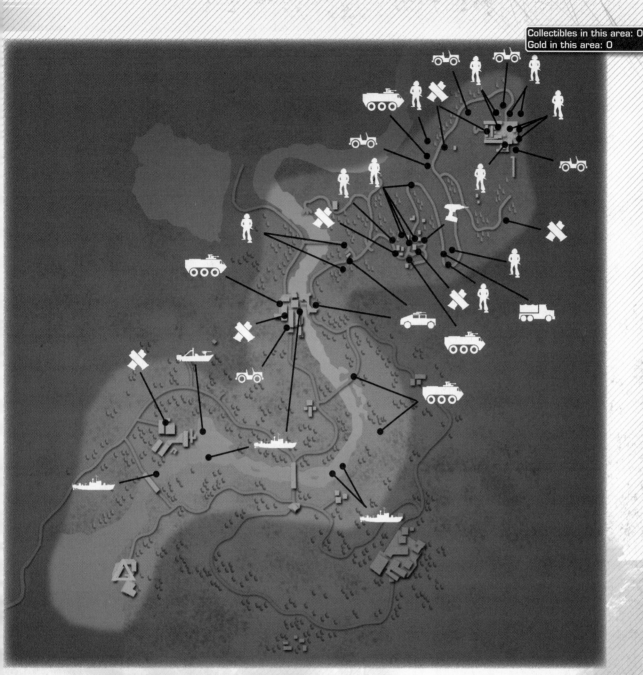

In the village, you have to eliminate an IFV...

up an M136 rocket launcher. Using buildings for cover, fire two rockets at the IFV to destroy it. Your next target is the helicopter. This one is tough to shoot down. Don't try to zoom in on it. Instead, use the targeting dot for your sights. When it hovers to attack, fire a rocket. It only takes one hit to bring it crashing down. After catching your breath, clear out any nearby soldiers, heal yourself, and repair your vehicle with a power tool you can find in the village.

Continue driving right into the village. You come under fire from a helicopter gunship as well as soldiers and an IFV. Race to the south end of the village where you can pick

...and a helicopter gunship.

★ ★ **TIP** ★ ★

The fight in the village is very tough. Constantly watch your health and heal as needed. Also watch the minimap to see where the helicopter is. If you run out of rockets, there is an ammo box to the north for refills.

Welcome · Basic Training · Infantry · Vehicles · Campaign · Multiplayer · Appendix

Welcome to Bad Company | Acta non Verba | Crossing Over | Par for the Course | Air Force One | **Crash and Grab** | Ghost Town

The enemy is constantly blocking your escape routes.

while you keep the boat going. Expect soldiers with RPGs at all the bridges and dodge to one side or the other when you see a rocket inbound. The enemy also sends boats up the river to try to sink you. There is also a large patrol boat near the village where this mission began. As always, keep moving until you get to the docks at the southern end of the map.

Get to this base on the river and choose a vehicle.

Drive out of the village and head for the enemy base that is on both sides of the river. On the way, you have to fight an armored jeep along with its dismounted infantry. Kill them all and keep moving. When you get to the base, you have several options. On the opposite side of the river you can find a jeep and an IFV. However, the quickest way to get to safety is by boat. Hop into a boat and take off down the river.

Bridges and patrol boats are best avoided with speed. Don't stop to take shots or you are a sitting duck.

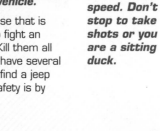

Keep the boat at full throttle and be careful not to hit the rocks as you drive over fords.

IFVs attack from the river banks.

The key to making your escape is to keep moving fast. Along the banks, soldiers and vehicles fire on you. Don't worry about fighting back. Your squad mans the weapons

At the docks, rescue Serdar from the Legionnaire's men who are about to kill him.

GHOST TOWN

Serdar kept his promise to show us where the Legionnaire's cargo ship sailed. We arrived near the coastal city of Sadiz. This city was supposed to be a great resort, however it was never finished. Now the Legionnaire is using it for a base of operations. Since Serdar has had enough trouble with the Legionnaire and his mercenaries, he chose to go into exile on his very own island. The gold only has to be split four ways now.

Collectibles in this mission: 7
Gold in this mission: 5

★ REACH SADIZ ★

MAKE YOUR WAY AROUND THE BAY TO REACH THE LEGIONNAIRE'S CARGO SHIP.

- ELIMINATE ALL ENEMIES
- REGROUP AT THE SMOKE
- ADVANCE TOWARD SADIZ
- DESTROY THE TWO BRIDGES
- ADVANCE TOWARD SADIZ

ELIMINATE ALL ENEMIES

Head east to get to the first enemy position.

Collectibles in this area: 1
Gold in this area: 0

PRIMA Official Game Guide

BAD COMPANY
BATTLEFIELD

Welcome · Basic Training · Infantry · Vehicles · **Campaign** · Multiplayer · Appendix

Welcome to Bad Company | Acta non Verba | Crossing Over | Par for the Course | Air Force One | Crash and Grab | **Ghost Town**

Since the docks where the cargo ship is are heavily defended against a naval assault, Bad Company will make a ground attack. To do this, you and your squad mates land on the beach to the east of the dock and must make your way around the bay to come at the dock from the landward side. Once your feet are on dry ground, start heading east toward the enemy's first base around the bay. The main path leads right into the small village. However, the enemy has lots of defenses and most of them can fire at this entrance to the village.

Climb up the hills to the south of the entrance and you can see all the snipers and weapons positions on the rooftops.

Start heading up the hill to the south of the village. Stay crouched to get a good view of the enemy defenses before the shooting starts. There is not a lot of cover on the hill. However, keep advancing to the east until you come across some trees. Large rocks at this position provide good cover. When you need to heal or reload, just crouch down. Your first target should be the rocket launcher on the rooftop to the north, followed by the machine gun on the rooftop to the northeast. Then go after the other enemies on the rooftops as well as those at ground level.

This spot by the trees is a good place for starting the attack. The rock provides some cover for you.

Pick up this M2CG rocket launcher.

An armored jeep drives down the road toward you. Eliminate it.

Once you have caused as much damage as you can from your hill position, sprint down into the village. If you head almost due north, pick up an M2CG rocket launcher left in a shed near the western entrance. This comes in handy against an armored jeep that comes down the street from the east. By this time, you can probably use some ammo. An ammo box outside the building with the rocket launcher on top fills you up.

Use the grenade launcher on your assault rifle to blow holes in the buildings to get the enemies hiding inside.

Scratch one tank.

Work your way around the village, clearing it of enemies. Many of the soldiers hide in the buildings, so blow holes in the structures with your grenade launcher. Your minimap is a great tool to locate these hidden enemies. Eventually a tank enters the village. Use the rocket launcher to take it out. Be sure to take cover behind buildings in between shots or the tank's weapons make short work of you.

★ TIP ★

While the rocket launcher is one way to take out the enemy tank, there are other ways as well. One is to use a tank of your own. You did not bring your own tank, but there is an empty tank in the eastern part of the village. When the enemy tank arrives, sprint to the empty tank and hop in. Then use this tank to destroy the enemy armor.

REGROUP AT THE SMOKE

Meet up with your squad at the smoke.

After you have eliminated all of the enemies in this area, you are ordered to meet up with your squad at the smoke. However, before you do, take some time to explore the village. Pick up an AUG assault rifle on the rooftop near the smoke and add this weapon to your collectibles. You can also find an XM8 light machine gun, some C4, and a power tool. If you plan on using the tank, take the power tool. Otherwise, stick with the rocket launcher. Be sure to visit the ammo box to load up, then walk to the red smoke.

Collectibles in this area: 3
Gold in this area: 2

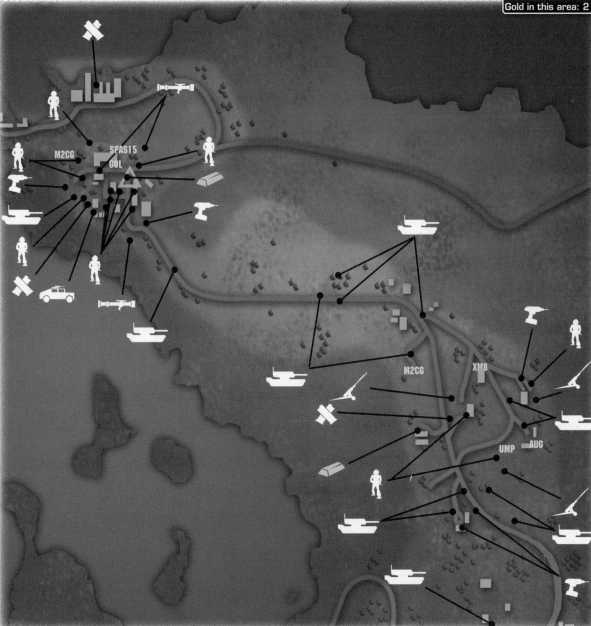

Head up this trail south of the village and quickly take out the soldier manning the rocket launcher.

Your new orders are to advance toward Sadiz. In order to progress toward your objective, you first have to go through another base. This one is just to the south of the village and located up on the hilltop. There are two ways to advance. The first is to go on foot, and the second involves driving a tank into battle. Let's look at the foot strategy first. Near where the tank and jeep are parked, a trail leads up to the next base.

Follow it to the top where you find a soldier manning a rocket launcher. Quickly kill him. Then use the rocket launcher if you want to start firing at enemies in the buildings by blowing holes in the walls as well as the soldiers. Fire the rifle and grenade launcher to finish up the job. There are two more rocket launchers in the base, so be sure to kill their gunners before they kill you.

Pick up this GOL sniper rifle and use it to clear out this area.

PRIMA Official Game Guide

BATTLEFIELD BAD COMPANY

Welcome • Basic Training • Infantry • Vehicles • Campaign • Multiplayer • Appendix

Welcome to Bad Company | Acta non Verba | Crossing Over | Par for the Course | Air Force One | Crash and Grab | Ghost Town

Explore the buildings to find a couple collectibles. The SPAS15 is a semi-automatic shotgun that is great for close quarters combat, while the GOL sniper rifle is best for long-range fire. Since you will do a lot of combat at range, pick up the GOL and use it to clear out the rest of the base, including the soldier hiding by the tank in the southwestern part of this site.

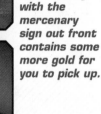

This building with the mercenary sign out front contains some more gold for you to pick up.

Finally, make your way to the southeastern two-story building. Recognize that sign outside? With the mercenary symbol and motto, it might as well say "Gold Here!" Go inside and help yourself. As you are moving around the southeastern part of the base, watch for an enemy tank to appear from the southeast. Use a tank or rocket launcher to destroy it before it harms your squad.

Drive along the road to the base on top of the hill.

If you decided to ride into combat in the tank, you won't be able to drive up the trail. Instead, follow the road that leads to the east, then turns around to the west to enter the base. Kill the soldier manning

Be sure to silence the rocket launcher at the entrance to the base.

the rocket launcher at the entrance and look for other enemies with rocket launchers or RPGs. They are your priority targets. Then you can just roll into the base and use the tank's cannon to bombard the buildings and clear them out.

Since you come under a lot of fire early in the attack and take damage, be ready to jump out and repair the tank with your power tool. Just remember to pop smoke from the tank to give you some concealment while you fix the damage.

Follow the road up this hill and be ready to take on three tanks at the same time.

When you are ready to continue on toward Sadiz, be sure to have a power tool and a fully repaired tank. Follow the road southeast up a hill. Once you get to the top and turn due east, be ready for some action. An enemy tank is directly ahead. Engage it quickly and destroy it since two more will arrive shortly—one from the right and the other from the left. If necessary, put your tank into reverse as you fire at them to make it harder for the enemies to hit your tank. After you have destroyed all three of these tanks, take the time to repair any damage since you will be going against more tanks shortly.

Continue following the road as it begins to turn to the south. As you advance, more enemy tanks come after you. When faced with more than one tank, focus on the closest one and keep firing at it until it

There are several more tanks in the open area to the south.

is destroyed. Then switch to another target. If you lose your tank, there is an M2CG rocket launcher in a dug out position west of the road as well as two available tanks—one in the south and the other in the east.

There are some artillery guns in this area firing on the U.S. forces. Destroy the artillery guns, or at least kill the soldiers manning them, or they fire on you as you advance south.

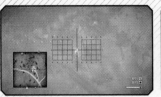

Take control of one of these guns and use it to destroy other artillery guns or even tanks—using the same targeting system you used during the first mission.

In addition to the tanks, there are also three artillery guns in the area. They are firing on the U.S. armor to the south. It is a very good idea to silence these guns or they will bombard you as you move south. Each gun is usually operated by a single soldier, so just kill him and the gun will no longer be a threat. You can also use these guns yourself. Climb onto one, target enemy tanks to the south, and take them out with an artillery barrage. After clearing out the tanks and artillery in this area, be sure to do some exploring. You can pick up assault rifles and even a UMP submachine gun for another collectible if you don't already have one. In addition, there is gold in some barracks along the western side of the road. Be sure to stop on by and enrich yourself even more.

*This small base in the east not only has a tank you can use, but also an **AUG** assault rifle and a **UMP** submachine gun.*

Don't forget to stop by these barracks and pick up a gold bar.

Once you have all you want from this area, follow the road as it heads east and makes a wide turn to the south and back to the west. Up ahead you see some tanks coming at you. However, they are quickly destroyed by the U.S. artillery. While that is good news, the bad news is that you are driving around in an enemy tank—it is only a short time before your tank is destroyed as well.

The U.S. artillery took out a bunch of enemy tanks. Yours is next.

DESTROY THE TWO BRIDGES

MAP ON NEXT PAGE

You have to get through this town to the bridges before the U.S. tanks.

Pick up some C4 to blow the bridges.

The U.S. Army is moving toward Sadiz. If they get there before you, they get the gold. Therefore, you need to find some way to delay them. In order to get to Sadiz, the U.S. tanks must cross a river.

There are two bridges on the other side of the town. If you can blow up both bridges, the tanks have to divert to another crossing. This objective is timed in that you have to blow the bridges before the tanks get to them. Since the tanks travel along the northern road through the town, the north bridge is the first one you need to destroy. To begin, run west to a fence overlooking the town. There is a machine gun on the rooftop due west of your position. Kill the gunner before he sees and opens fire on you. Then rush down the hill to pick up some C4 which you need to destroy the bridges.

The town is filled with enemy soldiers. Therefore, stay to the north of the town to avoid unnecessary delays.

Since you don't have a lot of time to get to the bridges, you don't want to waste time fighting your way through the town. Therefore, from the C4 stash, run west to the edge of the mission area and then turn to continue southwest right at the edge of the town. You take some fire, but just heal as you keep moving. There is one soldier on a rooftop that you need to kill as you advance. However, by staying just outside of town, you bypass a lot of enemies and get to the bridge quicker.

PRIMA Official Game Guide

BAD COMPANY BATTLEFIELD

Welcome · Basic Training · Infantry · Vehicles · Campaign · Multiplayer · Appendix

Welcome to Bad Company | Acta non Verba | Crossing Over | Par for the Course | Air Force One | Crash and Grab | **Ghost Town**

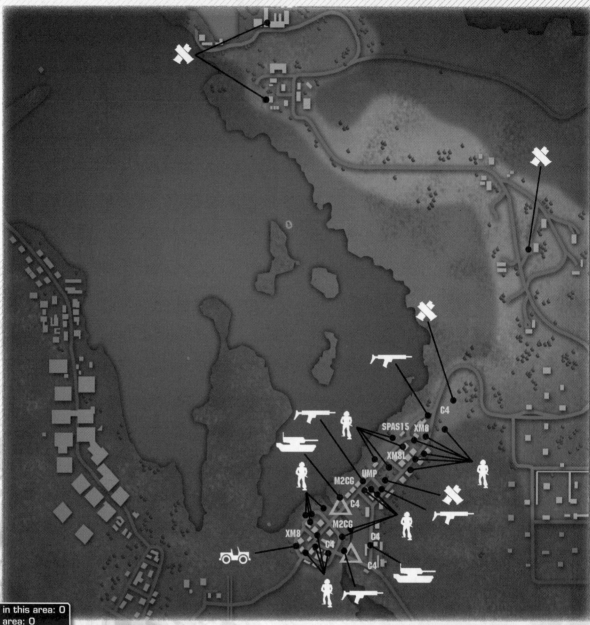

Collectibles in this area: 0
Gold in this area: 0

Place a C4 charge on the tank to destroy it.

Blow the first bridge.

As you approach the first bridge, there is a tank waiting to protect the bridge. Since you have C4 already, run up to the tank, place a charge, and then quickly move to cover and detonate it. One charge takes out the tank. There is also an M2CG rocket launcher in a building adjacent to the tank which you can pick up and use to destroy the tank if you don't want to get too close to it. Once the tank is a smoking wreck, run out onto the bridge, drop a C4 charge at the objective position, then run to the opposite side of the bridge and detonate. One bridge is down. One more to go.

Shoot this enemy located between the two bridges.

Once on the other side of the river, turn to the southeast and kill a soldier next to the river, standing between the two bridges. He is armed with a light machine gun and will cause a lot of injury to you unless you quickly

Use the rocket launcher to destroy the tank guarding the south bridge.

take him out. Advance to where he was standing, and pick up an M2CG rocket launcher. Another tank is guarding the south bridge and starts shooting at you. While dodging its main

gun rounds, fire a couple rockets into the tank to destroy it. Make sure you are fully healed, then rush out onto the south bridge and place a C4 charge. Get off the bridge and detonate it to complete your objectives and buy time to get to the gold before the Army does.

Just because you made it across the river and blew the bridges, you are not yet out of the fire. There are more enemies on this side of the river that try to kill you. Since the timed part of the mission is over,

Destroy the enemy jeep in the western part of the town.

take your time and advance through this section of the town. You can pick up an XM8 assault rifle here if you need one. If you don't have an assault rifle at this point in the mission, be sure to get one. The grenade launcher will come in handy. The enemy also has a jeep in this area. Shoot the gunners first or fire grenades at it to prevent this vehicle from killing you.

ADVANCE TOWARD SADIZ

MAP ON NEXT PAGE

Take out the soldiers manning the two machine guns.

As you progress toward Sadiz, your route has you following a road. Since the road is well defended, head up onto the ridge running along the right side of the road and move while crouched down. There are

Before going under the pipeline, shoot the enemies on the rooftop of the building on the other side.

a couple machine guns guarding the road, and from the high position on the ridge, you can kill both gunners before they put the hurt on you. There are also a couple other soldiers between you and the pipeline. In addition, you can also see a couple soldiers on the other side of the pipeline. They are located on the rooftop and one is armed with an RPG. Shoot the soldiers on the other side of the pipeline while you are still on the ridge.

There is gold located on the right side of this building. Clear the building out first, then get your reward.

As you cross under the pipeline, be ready to launch a grenade of your own at the enemy grenade launcher located on the left end of the building. Once the building is clear, walk around to the right side to find a mercenary case with a gold bar for you to take. If you search the area, you can also find a GOL sniper rifle and an XM8 light machine gun. While the light machine gun is an option, don't take the sniper rifle for now since you will be fighting at close ranges during the next engagements. Now advance up a ridge line to some red smoke and Miss July will inform you of a surprise.

Continue to the red smoke to get your next set of orders.

BAD COMPANY
BATTLEFIELD

Welcome · Basic Training · Infantry · Vehicles · Campaign · Multiplayer · Appendix

Welcome to Bad Company | Acta non Verba | Crossing Over | Par for the Course | Air Force One | Crash and Grab | **Ghost Town**

Collectibles in this area: 0
Gold in this area: 1

REACH THE GOLD

HURRY TO JOIN UP WITH SARGE AND
SWEETWATER BY THE CARGO SHIP.

▸ PICK UP SUPPLIES　　▸ USE LASER DESIGNATOR ON THE SILO　　▸ MOVE OUT　　▸ LOCATE TRANSPORT　　▸ JEEP RIDE

PICK UP SUPPLIES

The supply drop is on the rooftop of a building.

Pick up an M2CG rocket launcher while it is quiet.

120

Collectibles in this area: 3
Gold in this area: 1

QJU88

M2CG   C4

LZ-537

M2CG

9A91

1194

Miss July contacts your squad and lets you know she has had some supplies dropped for you to use. These supplies are located on a rooftop of a building to the west of your location. Red smoke marks the spot to make it easier for you to see. At this point in the mission, Sarge and Sweetwater are moving ahead to the cargo ship while you and Haggard get the supplies. However, before going directly to the supplies, stop by a building at the edge of this city and pick up an M2CG rocket launcher. You will need it later, so you might as well pick it up now. As you advance to the objective building, don't worry about any enemies. There are none right now. To get to the rooftop, enter the building and climb up the stairs to the second floor. Then move out onto the balcony and climb a ladder to the roof. The supplies consist of a LZ-537 laser designator.

Pick up the laser designator and get ready for your next order.

PRiMA Official Game Guide

BATTLEFIELD BAD COMPANY

Welcome · Basic Training · Infantry · Vehicles · Campaign · Multiplayer · Appendix

Welcome to Bad Company | Acta non Verba | Crossing Over | Par for the Course | Air Force One | Crash and Grab | **Ghost Town**

USE LASER DESIGNATOR ON THE SILO

This large silo is your target.

Guide the bomb right onto the silo.

Once you pick up the laser designator, you get orders to blow up a silo to the south of your position. Take aim and get a lock on the structure. Then once the airplane drops the bomb, guide it right onto the silo to create a huge explosion and complete this objective.

MOVE OUT

Use the laser designator to take out a couple tanks that threaten you.

After the silo blows up, the mercenaries move in to take you out. Be ready to shoot a couple mercs in the building to the south. Stay low and kill them. Enemy tanks are also sent in to hunt you down. One arrives from the south. Use the laser designator to destroy it as well as another to the north of your building. Stay on the rooftop and away from the edges while engaging these two tanks.

Shoot the mercenaries down below from your rooftop position.

Once both tanks are destroyed, pick up the M2CG rocket launcher, then use your rifle to start killing mercenaries moving around below you. You can clear out several without leaving the rooftop. After neutralizing all that you can, head down to the ground level and begin searching the area for collectible weapons. As you are moving about, watch for a tank to the north as well as more mercenaries. There is an ammo box in the middle of the area where you can fill up for this fight and the next engagement.

There are three collectible weapons in this area, so be sure to pick them all up.

★ TIP ★

You can get a QJU88 light machine gun, a 9A91, and a T194 all within buildings in this area. If you have been diligent in the past missions about getting all of these types of weapons, with the addition of these three, you will have a complete collection.

Use the rocket launcher to destroy this tank in the north.

The last tank in this area is located near a checkpoint leading into Sadiz. Use your M2CG rocket launcher to destroy it. After you have cleared the area of all mercenaries, move to a building in the northwest and climb a ladder up to the roof to find a case with a gold bar. Once you have it, move to the checkpoint to continue the mission.

The gold in this area is on a rooftop of a building located in the northwest corner.

Collectibles in this area: 0
Gold in this area: 0

VSS

GOL

GOL

M2GC

As you approach the new and unfinished part of Sadiz, the Legionnaire takes off in his helicopter. However, he has left a lot of surprises for you in this area.

Watch for lots of snipers in the upper levels of this area.

PRIMA Official Game Guide

BAD COMPANY
BATTLEFIELD

Welcome · Basic Training · Infantry · Vehicles · **Campaign** · Multiplayer · Appendix

Welcome to Bad Company | Acta non Verba | Crossing Over | Par for the Course | Air Force One | Crash and Grab | **Ghost Town**

This next area through which you must advance is full of mercenaries on the ground and snipers on the upper levels. Always move from cover to cover and be ready to heal yourself. A good strategy is to try and engage as many of the enemies as you approach the large buildings still under construction. This prevents you from being surrounded and attacked by several soldiers at the same time.

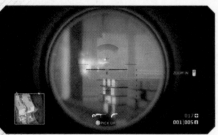

As you are advancing through this area, the U.S. Army begins an artillery bombardment. These rounds hurt you as well as the enemy, so stay inside the buildings for protection. While you want to stay

Watch out for a couple tanks in this area. Use your rocket launcher to take them out.

to the northeastern part of this area, there is a tank in the north you have to destroy. Find an interior wall to hide behind, then move out from behind it to shoot a rocket. Quickly move back behind the wall to reload. Interior walls can't be destroyed and therefore make great cover against a tank. Another tank is located to the west, so try to take it out as well. There are a couple of sniper rifles in this area you can pick up; however, you are better off sticking with an assault rifle. Keep advancing toward the north and you see several vehicles which could take you to the rest of your squad.

Don't try to run to these tanks and climb in. The artillery destroys them before you can get there.

JEEP RIDE

Collectibles in this area: 0
Gold in this area: 1

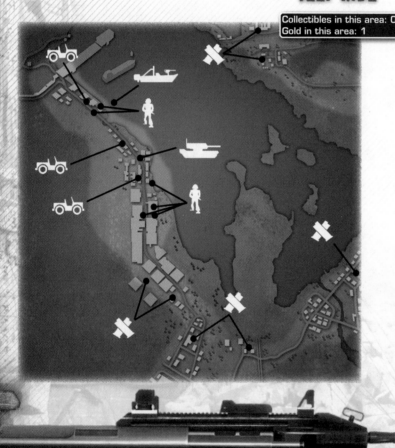

The gold bar can be found near the swimming pools.

As you approach the vehicles, the artillery wipes them all out except for a jeep. However, before approaching the jeep, locate a couple of empty swimming pools. Right next to them the mercenaries have left one of their cases. Open it and take a gold bar. This is the final individual gold bar. If you have been careful to collect each of them during the missions, you will have all of them once you pick up this one. Now head for the jeep. Haggard offers to drive this time, so just enjoy the ride as you man the grenade launcher.

Haggard is already waiting for you in the jeep.

Haggard takes you for a wild and crazy ride through Sadiz. You have to ride past soldiers with RPGs, tanks, enemy jeeps, and even a patrol boat.

When you meet up with Sarge and Sweetwater, you see that they have found the gold. However, the Legionnaire does not seem like the type of guy to let anyone take his property without a fight.

⭐ DEFEND THE GOLD ⭐

 **KILL THE LEGIONNAIRE.**

▸ REACH THE ANTI-AIRCRAFT GUN ▸ TAKE DOWN THE LEGIONNAIRE

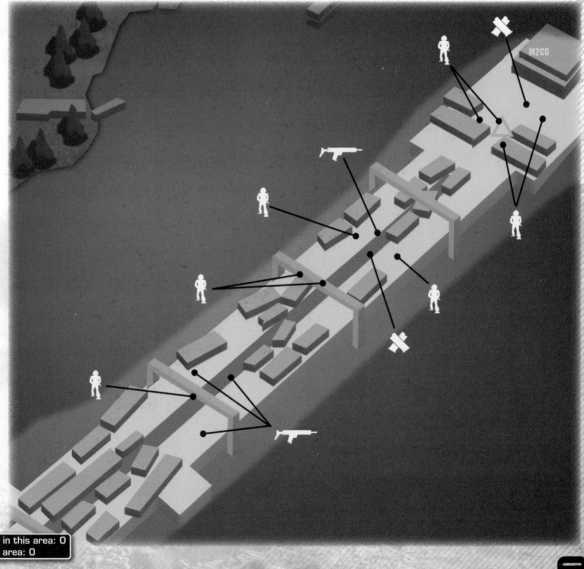

Collectibles in this area: 0
Gold in this area: 0

PRIMA Official Game Guide

BATTLEFIELD BAD COMPANY

Welcome · Basic Training · Infantry · Vehicles · Campaign · Multiplayer · Appendix

Welcome to Bad Company | Acta non Verba | Crossing Over | Par for the Course | Air Force One | Crash and Grab | Ghost Town

REACH THE ANTI-AIRCRAFT GUN

Shoot the soldiers manning the machine guns as well as those on the catwalks above the pier.

Pick up assault rifle ammo from the dead mercenaries.

The Legionnaire is attacking you with his helicopter. Sweetwater suggests using the anti-aircraft gun on the pier to shoot him down. However, you have to fight your way through mercenaries to get to the gun. Make your way down the pier toward the gun. The main threat are three machine guns about halfway down the pier. Because of all the objects on the pier, you are only exposed to the fire of one machine gun. Take aim at the soldier manning the gun and kill him. Then move forward and hit the soldiers at the other two guns from their flank where they can't use their machine gun to attack you. There are also mercenaries up on the catwalks that like to shoot down at you. Of course, while you are fighting the mercenaries, the Legionnaire is strafing you, so be quick to heal whenever you take damage.

The anti-aircraft gun is at the top of this ramp. However, as you approach it, the gun blows up.

Get advancing cautiously down the pier. Eventually you see the anti-aircraft gun up on a platform. There are some mercenaries behind sandbags guarding it, so take them out, then move up the ramp to man the gun. Just as you get to the gun, it blows up. You will have to find another way to shoot down the Legionnaire.

TAKE DOWN THE LEGIONNAIRE

Climb up the stairs to pick up an M2CG rocket launcher on the upper deck at the end of the pier.

The best weapon for the job is a rocket launcher. You should still have one from before, but if you don't, climb up the stairs to the upper platform and find a rocket launcher off to one side. Pick it up, then head back down the stairs to the level where the anti-aircraft gun was located.

The Legionnaire fires rockets at you as he makes his attack runs. Try to move out of the way if you can.

Wait to fire until the Legionnaire pulls the nose of his helicopter up and hovers momentarily.

Since you can't guide the rockets, it can be tough to shoot down the Legionnaire. He will be attacking you constantly, so try to move away as his rockets are headed your way. Heal frequently to avoid being killed by the intense barrages. If you stay on the second deck, you have an ammo box nearby where you can get more rockets. It takes two hits to bring down this helicopter, so make sure every shot counts. The best time to fire is when the helicopter is hovering with its underside facing toward you. The Legionnaire pulls this maneuver after each attack run to prepare for the next. Just wait for this opportunity and get in your two shots to bring this enemy down.

The Legionnaire has been shot down.

It looks like the Army arrived and is hauling away the gold.

An officer orders your squad to drive a truck filled with a load of gold as a part of a convoy.

As you bring up the rear of the convoy, your truck takes a detour. Bad Company finally got its reward.

However, it appears someone did not die in a fiery helicopter crash. And he does not look happy about losing his gold.

PRIMA Official Game Guide

BATTLEFIELD BAD COMPANY

MULTIPLAYER

While the single-player campaign is a great adventure full of fun, it is only half of the game. The multiplayer experience is the other half. Playing against other humans and working together as a team with the members of your squad adds an entirely new dimension of fun.

THE BASICS

When playing a multiplayer game, there are a few things you need to do to get started. There are also some differences in the way you play. Let's take a quick look at the nuances of multiplayer games to make your experience enjoyable.

STARTING A GAME

Once you get to the multiplayer menu, you can choose to play a quickmatch or a custom match. Quickmatches put you in the first available multiplayer game. You do not get any choice in which game you will be in; however, it is the quickest way to play. Custom matches let you choose which map you would like to play as well as the challenge level of the game—either normal or hard. In addition, custom matches allow you to form a squad. Before you get into a game, you can invite up to three of your friends to join with you. Then, when you start or join a custom game, you will all be together on the same team and in the same squad.

COMMUNICATION

Multiplayer games are always team versus team. You are never on your own. If you want to win, you need to communicate with the other players. During a game, you can communicate via your headset with the other members of your squad. There may be more players on your team, assigned to different squads; however, you can only communicate with the players in your own squad. In addition to chatting about the weather, it is important to keep your squad mates apprised of your situation. Call out enemies that you see or warn them of threats. Before you launch a grenade or detonate an explosive charge, let your squad know so they won't get in the way or be killed by your action. Communication is the key to the next topic, playing as a team.

PLAYING AS A TEAM

Within a squad, players should select different classes to take on different roles. A squad of all one class is not very flexible. Instead, your squad should have some variety to it. For example, one member could be a recon class soldier and stay back to provide sniper support for the rest of the squad. One member should select the Demolition kit to help deal with enemy vehicles and positions. There should be a support class soldier to help heal wounds and repair vehicles. In addition, by including different types of kits, your squad gains access to the different unlockable items. A squad only needs one laser designator or mortar strike.

One of the useful features is the squad spawn ability. When you die, you have the choice of spawning at your base or spawning near your squad. If your squad is deep in enemy territory, the squad spawn can put you right into the action without having to travel the length of the map. While playing, you will get a message that you are the last one of your squad alive if all the other members have been killed. Immediately take cover to give your squad mates a chance to spawn near your location or the entire squad has to start back at the base.

Another important part of playing as a team is to coordinate the actions of the squad. For example, if you are going to run across an open area, make sure at least one of your squad is covering you—waiting for an enemy to pop up to shoot you. Then, once you get to a position with cover, you can support your squad mates as they cross the open terrain.

FOCUS ON THE OBJECTIVE

To win a multiplayer game, it is vital that you focus on the objective. While killing enemies is your main task, you need to remember what objective must be completed to win the game. The objective dictates all of your actions. Your movement is to get to the objective. When you engage enemies, it is either to defend your objective or clear a path to the objective for your squad.

GOLD RUSH

Battlefield: Bad Company offers a single game mode initially—Gold Rush. In this type of game, one team is the attacker while the other is the defender. On the map are several bases controlled by the defender. The attacker's objective is to destroy all of the enemy bases. The bases consist of two crates filled with gold. Once both crates have been destroyed, that base is considered destroyed and the defender receives a new base to defend with two more gold crates. This new base is farther away from the original front lines. The attacker has a certain number of tickets at the beginning of a mission. Whenever an attacking soldier dies, it costs a ticket for the soldier to respawn on the map. Once the tickets run out, the attackers can't spawn any killed soldiers back onto the map. However, once the attacker destroys a base, the team gets more tickets and possibly more vehicles as well. The defenders do not have to worry about tickets. They have an unlimited number of respawns. The defender wins by eliminating all attackers and reducing their tickets to zero so they can't spawn back into the game.

ASCENSION

This is a tough, infantry-focused map. Ascension leads upward from a hilltop village to an imposing monastery. You fight through backyards and winding streets before the battle culminates in the twisting dark corridors of the monastery.

BASE 1

Attackers come under fire from the defenders almost immediately. As an attacker, you will understand the value of having a higher firing position. Watch for defenders covering the courtyard from the buildings. The crate in the house is well covered and there is no easy way to get in. But remember, you can blow the walls, which will often take the defenders by surprise.

Defenders, you need to be disciplined here. Cover attack routes and watch the crates, but don't be tempted to come down to the attacker's base. If a squad gets in behind you, the whole base can fall like a house of cards. Watch for the attackers bringing the vehicle up and steal it if you can—it works just as well as a defensive gun platform.

BASE 2

For the attackers, once base 1 goes, it is really important to mop up stragglers. They can do a lot of damage from behind. Try to create new routes through the houses. Turning up somewhere unexpected can really disrupt the defense. Working as a squad is critical here and can yield great success. Watch for stationary machine guns covering the routes.

Defenders, coordination is key. There are three main routes, but watch for attackers creating new ones through the houses. Use the machine guns. They're tempting targets, but they can take down lots of attackers before you lose them. If you are on one, spend a moment clearing some of the clutter out of the way to improve your view and firing angles.

BASE 3

This can be a real ordeal for the attackers. The monastery is an ancient building with extremely thick walls, so there are limited options for opening new routes. Use both entrances—the more sneaky side entrance as well as the main one. When inside, look for alternative routes. Sometimes taking the stairs up will bypass the defenders below.

PRIMA Official Game Guide

BAD COMPANY
BATTLEFIELD

Defenders, try to get back as quickly as possible when base 2 goes, even if that means taking yourself out to respawn at the third base. If you are set up before the attackers arrive, it is a lot easier to hold the base. Cover both entrances. The main entrance draws a lot of the action, but watch the side door, too. One of the areas that can be destroyed is the roof. Covering the courtyard from there often surprises attackers, but be aware that your route to the crates is that much longer.

Ascension gives some really intense combat and can feel quite chaotic. If you work as a group and coordinate your efforts, you will see the benefits.

DECONSTRUCTION

As the name suggests, this level takes place at a construction site being developed next to the water processing plant from Valley Run. The focal points of the map are the bridge and the large building sites at the end of the map, which provide very different fighting experiences.

ASAP. The defenders have a tank on the other side as well, so watch out. Get a foothold on the bridge by whatever means necessary and avoid getting drawn into a war of attrition across it.

Defenders should mop up attackers that make it over the bridge and be aware of them circling you. Remember that with squad spawn, one attacker becomes four very quickly.

BASE 1

Base 1 is located leading up to the bridge with the attackers swarming through the far side of the processing plant and up on the main blockaded road where the defenders await them. As an attacker, you'll probably come under attack pretty much from the get go. Working your way through the maze-like warehouses or taking cover behind the advancing light tank are good options.

As a defender, it can feel like shooting fish in a barrel. But be aware that if you can see them, they can see you—so mix up your vantage points. Keep an eye out for which crate is being attacked, then react to that.

BASE 2

Base 2 is the bridge. It is a classic bottleneck and can come at a high cost for the attacking team. The attacking team needs to get across as quickly as possible. Clear a route across for the tank

BASE 3

Base 3 is the construction yard. It is deceptively difficult for the attackers to take it down. It feels spread out, but it is easy for defenders to hole up and hold on. Attackers, vary your routes. There are many ways through from the bridge and it is easy for the defenders to cover them. But they can get fixated on one point and you can slip through. Remember, you may need to take down walls to get to the objectives. Try to arrive in numbers.

Defenders, be aware that attackers come at you from many directions. Try not to get too bunched up. There are many ambush points on the way through, but don't get drawn out too far from the objectives.

Deconstruction can really go either way. Attackers can make lightning strikes and push all the way through or the defenders can dig in and stop the advance at the first base. Each base has different dynamics, which varies the kind of game you need to play. Remember, though, fortune favors the bold.

On Final Ignition, you fight through a gas processing plant, often with explosive consequences. A mix of vehicle and infantry combat awaits you on this desert map, surrounded by refineries, silos, gantries, and containers.

BASE 1

As the attacker, advancing on foot, using the buildings for cover is an effective tactic. If using vehicles, advance up the road, but watch for laser designators and rockets fired from the roof of the factory. Make sure to keep the Bradley alive as the fire support it provides gives a significant advantage.

Sniping from the rooftop of the factory is a good strategy for defenders, but remember that when attackers get in, the recon class soldiers become less effective in close combat. Focus on keeping the tank out of the fight. If a support class soldier is repairing it, make sure to take that soldier down first.

BASE 2

Again, keeping the Bradley alive really helps the attackers on this base. Use it for fire support. Rushing in will get it taken out quickly. The gantries provide a quick route across, but you'll be very exposed. If you're a good sniper, provide cover from the factory. There are a lot of good sniper spots and you can cover both crates effectively.

As defenders, watch for attackers getting footholds on the roofs and your base. They can really wreak havoc. Keep the Bradley out of the game and watch for attackers advancing across the gantries or through the silos.

BASE 3

Crossing the bridges can be treacherous for attackers, even with the Abrams you now have. Keeping the Bradley alive and using that as a diversion often lets you sneak around with the Abrams across this less-obvious bridge. The Abrams takes out most things one on one, but watch out for massed forces.

When defending, keep an eye on the main bridge, but don't get too bunched. If the attackers get into the base courtyard, it can be tricky to retake it. The roof in the center of the compound is a strong defensive position. Support gunners can pin down infantry and the Stalkers can keep the Abrams at bay.

Final Ignition is a great mix of vehicle and infantry combat. Managing your vehicle resources is key. For those less inclined to play fair, stealing an opponent's tank can swing the balance in your favor.

HARVEST DAY

Harvest Day is a vehicle-oriented map. Here we have Russian armored forces advancing across lush fields, idyllic farms, and into the outskirts of a U.S.-held village.

BASE 1

If you're attacking, remember to flank. You have a field on one side and a wooded hill on the other. It is a lot harder for the defender to repel an attack from both sides.

If you are defending, a tactic you may want to try is to have your specialist sneak out to a little shed. From there, tag enemy vehicles as they advance past you and even set traps on the road with C4. Generally it gives you a good overview of where the attackers are coming from.

BASE 2

As an attacker, getting into the middle of the village can be tricky, not to mention dangerous. Again, remember that attacking on a wide front is often more effective. Crates can be shelled from long range and you still have the numeric advantage with tanks.

First thing for the defenders to do is blow that bridge. Attackers can still cross the ford right next to it, but taking the bridge out limits how attackers can advance. Watch for tanks on the other side of the river shelling from long range.

BASE 3

As an attacker, try to sneak up through the village. With squad spawn, it is a good way to take a base down quickly. If possible, take this crate down first, because it is easier to hit the other one from long range, which is a good use of the tanks.

As defender, you are light on vehicles, but have two very defensible houses. Cover each house. Selecting the demolitions class often works well. They have the best anti-tank capability plus the shotgun for when it gets up close and personal.

BASE 4

Attackers will want to press on quickly from the previous base. If the bridge goes, it is a lot more difficult. If on foot, try working your way around through the houses. While there is a lot of noise and smoke, it is often easier to slip in unnoticed.

As defenders, take the bridge out quickly. This limits the attackers' routes in so you can defend them more easily. Mines are often very useful here.

FINAL BASE

This can be tough for attackers if the defenders get organized. By now, the attackers have probably run out of vehicles, so it is a much more even fight, except the defenders have a height advantage. As an attacker, try to keep a tank alive and vary your attack path. You can get up through the forest on the left or attack from the front up the slope as well as going up the road.

For defenders, try to cover the approaches. The attackers come from three sides, so keep an eye on where the action is and be ready to respond if a charge gets planted on one of the crates.

Harvest Day is a favorite map, with a mix of vehicle and close-in fighting in a great looking, varied setting. Take some time to look around, but watch for the enemy while you are doing it.

OASIS

Following the course of a desert river, Oasis is one of the more vehicle-oriented maps in the game. For the second half of the action, however, the gameplay will funnel into built-up areas and take on a more close-quarters feel.

BASE 1

The attackers' material significantly outweighs the defenders in this first clash, and it is telling that you have both air and artillery support. Put both to good use and back your squad mates up. It is easy to forget teamwork when in vehicles and the large numbers can make you feel invincible. However, the anti-aircraft gun will make short work of the Apache and solitary tanks make inviting targets.

Defenders, this base is like being between the hammer and the anvil. By the time the onslaught is finished, there won't be much left standing. It can help to come out and meet the attackers

halfway. There are small outlying settlements where you can slow down the assault. Try to divert attention away from the crates and whittle down their numbers.

BASE 2

You still have plenty of vehicles here as the attacker, but the playing field is a lot more even now. Don't expect to steamroll this base the same way as the previous one. Try to keep as much alive from base one as possible—especially heavy tanks. They can make a big difference later. Often it is easier to shoot the crates from long range instead of placing charges.

Defenders, you have a more even spread of vehicles this time, so it is a better balanced experience. As always, try not to get too drawn out and watch for individual attacks on the crates. Also watch for attackers skirting behind you. They can take you by surprise and cause havoc.

BASE 3

The crates are spread out, so attackers can choose to concentrate on one crate at a time or spread their forces. Supporting the attack with any tanks kept alive makes this much easier. Watch if the enemy has kept the helicopter from the last base. It can really hurt you since you have no real anti-aircraft support.

Defenders, you're short on vehicles again. Try to keep them alive from the previous base—especially the helicopter. Watch how the attackers are spreading their strike and try to react. It is difficult to hold both crates, so sometimes concentrating on one can help.

PRIMA Official Game Guide

BAD COMPANY BATTLEFIELD

BASE 4

The bases are spread out again and built up, so watch for defender ambushes. Assaulting one crate at a time often works well, but watch out for the crossfire on the open streets. Working around behind can be a good tactic and often surprises defenders more than taking more central routes.

The attackers are probably running low on vehicles now, but as a defender, prioritize taking out any remaining enemy tanks. The area is built up, so set up ambush points, but watch out for attackers flanking you. Use the rooftops to your best advantage. Attackers tend to arrive on ground level.

FINAL BASE

This one can be very difficult for the attackers to get into. If possible, coordinate attacks using the tank and infantry and try not to arrive always using the same route. Take out one crate at a time. Though exposed, the one in the square can be defended very easily. For the raised crate, remember that there are a few routes up.

Defenders, concentrate defense on the crate in the square. Take cover in buildings and pick off attackers as they try to run in. Watch out for attackers driving around with the tank or using boats. Dig in properly here, and even though the rest of the map has gone against you, you can turn the tide.

Oasis has a variety of playing areas, each of which requires a different approach. Protecting your vehicle resources pays off and can make all the difference in the later stages.

OVER AND OUT

Over and Out is the second part of Harvest Day and has more of an infantry focus. The map progresses through the remains of the village, out past some castle ruins, and culminates in an intense battle in a secluded communications center nestled in the forest. The map is characterized by some pretty intense close-quarters fighting in a couple of areas, so be prepared to get your hands dirty.

BASE 1

This is the most open area and there is some fighting across the bridge over the river. Attackers, fighting directly across the bridge can be really dangerous, so try to cross in force and also vary the attack a bit. It is easy for the defenders to get holed up, so you need to break them open as much as possible. If there is a stalemate, remember that the crates can be shot from long range.

For the defenders, be prepared to cover multiple routes. Attackers are going to come across rickety bridges. A good idea is to snipe from the rear

house, but it has a blind spot. You will need to change up from time to time. Watch for attackers working their way around to your back.

BASE 2

This takes you into the castle ruins. This can be a really intense area with a lot of close-in fighting, so if you want dog tags, this is the place for you. The castle ruins themselves are indestructible, so they are not going to change their shape during the course of the combat. Attackers, working your way straight up the hill can be tricky. If the defenders dig in, you can have a hard time here.

Squad spawn is very important, so stick together and watch each other's backs. Try using C4 so you don't trip the alarms, but watch out for your squad mates when you set them off. Also, you can often work your way through the left-hand side of the area. With all the action going on by the ruins, you can often slip through undetected.

Defenders, initially this is going to feel like a turkey shoot, but remember that the tables can turn quickly. Don't be tempted to come too far down the hill. If the attackers get in behind you, the base will fall quickly. Keep an eye on both objectives. Also, if you see one going, throw a grenade into the location. You are going to damage the objective, but often you take out a whole squad.

BASE 3

For the section leading up to the final communications center, it is a good idea for the defender to set up ambushes, because the attackers will be focused on getting to the communications center. You can try to stage an ambush here, but mostly as a delaying tactic, since you don't want the attacker to get too far ahead of you.

The communications center itself is fairly open, but it tightens up when you get close to the objectives. Attackers, be wary of those ambushes along the road up. Also, try to focus on one base at a time, taking out the stationary weapons for each one. On the communications center itself, try to attack from both sides. The defenders are going to be able to set up defenses easily in the basement, so watch yourself.

Over and Out is one of the more intense experiences in the game. The map progresses nicely for each zone. Watch each other's back out there. Work as a team and you should be able to crack what is a tough nut for both sides.

Valley Run is one of the tighter of the vehicle-oriented maps, so the side with the vehicles won't necessarily have the advantage. The level itself follows the course of a river upstream. It passes a communications center and then moves onward toward a water processing plant.

BASE 1

The gatehouse of the complex is a natural bottleneck for the defenders to set up shop. Attackers, use the vehicle advantage that you have. Try also looking for routes through the woods as well as along the road and remember that you have a boat you can flank with, too. For the first few bases, you are going to have artillery that can soften up the attack, but remember to watch out for your teammates.

Defenders, the opening here is wide, but it is easily defended as well. Also watch for attackers trying flank you.

BASE 2

This base is set back from the road and has lots of defenses, but there are a many routes across the river. Holding both entrances to the communications center simultaneously is going to be very hard for the defenders.

Attackers, vary your attack route. Watch out for the bridge. There is a lot of cover there for the defenders to set up ambushes for you on the far side. Take a look at the minimap and check out where the combat is focused. If it is centered around one of the gold crates, you can sometimes slip through and take out the other one unnoticed.

Defenders, there are a number of ambush points here, both across the river and over the bridge, so use a lot of anti-tank mines and C4. The communications center itself is a real fortress, so try to hold on to it for as long as possible.

PRIMA Official Game Guide

BAD COMPANY
BATTLEFIELD

BASE 3

This is more of a holding point for the defenders. There is not a great deal of hard cover for you here. If combat persists, this place is going to get worn down. Attackers, it is easy to get drawn into a pounding match here, but remember that the defenders have got nothing to lose in terms of lives, so they have the winning advantage on that one.

Defenders, there are not a lot of routes, but there is a lot of visual cover. Try to mix the team up with short- and long-range kits, but remember that the attackers can quite often appear from behind you.

BASE 4

This is where the defenders get their own armor, but the entrance is wider than it looks and the crates are separated by a lot of distance. Attackers, be prepared for the defenders to try to exit the base—especially with their tank. You can sometimes work around the side, up the river, or through the forests.

Defenders, try not to get too far drawn out. If the BMD-3 is in the courtyard, it can perform a very successful damage limitation role by reacting to the crates under attack.

BASE 5

This is much more tricky for the attacker, because there are a lot of wide open spaces and cover for the defenders. Try to get the BMD-3 over the bridge. It can provide good fire support when you get over there.

Defenders, be wary of single players crossing over. There is a lot of visual cover, but that can work both ways. And if there is a good attacking squad, it can be difficult to dislodge.

That is Valley Run, atmospheric and intense enough to balance on a knife edge. Explore the alternate routes. Perhaps there is more here than meets the eye.

★ SCORING ★

During multiplayer games, you earn points which count toward the online ranking system. Your total score for a round is the combined sum of both your general score as well as bonus points. For example, you could earn points for a kill, plus the bonus points if it was a headshot. Let's take a look at the points you earn for various actions.

GENERAL SCORING

KILL SCORING

Action	Points
Kill	10
Trace (If a player fires a tracer on to an enemy and a teammate hits the enemy)	3
Team kill	-15
Team damage (>50% damage)	-10
Team vehicle damage (>50% damage)	-10

TEAMWORK SCORING

Action	Points
Assisting from vehicle (passengers mounted on guns in vehicle gets small share of kills)	5
Heal (points given when healing 50% on any team member)	10
Repair vehicle (whenever repairing friendly vehicles with more than 50% damage)	10
Kill assist (caused >20% health damage prior to other player's kill)	3
Driver assist (drivers get bonus points for other players' kills from vehicle)	5
Destroy hot vehicle (destroy recently occupied enemy vehicles, within a few seconds)	10

BONUS POINTS

GENERAL BONUSES

Action	Points
Headshot	5
Savior point (killing an enemy while he/she is wounding one of your teammates)	5
Avenger point (killing an enemy when he/she has killed one of your teammates)	5
Damaging the objective (as attacker when causing 25% of damage on the objective)	10
Destroying the objective (as attacker when planting the bomb and having it detonate)	30
Defend bonus (killing enemies within a radius of the objective)	3

SQUAD MEMBER BONUSES

Action	Points
Heal a squad member	5
Repair a vehicle with a squad member inside	5
Pick up a squad member	1

Action	Points
Driver assist (for squad member kills in driver's vehicle)	3
Kill assist (cause >50% health damage prior to other player's kill)	3

As you earn points, you will be promoted in rank. In addition to earning points through scoring, you can also receive additional points when you earn awards. Awards are discussed later in this chapter. Promotion to some ranks allow you to unlock an item or weapon. This table shows the order of the ranks along with the number of points needed for promotion and whether you receive an unlock or not.

Rank name	Points	Unlock	
1. Private	100	Yes	
2. Private First Class	330	Yes	
3. Specialist	630	No	
4. Corporal	1000	Yes	
5. Sergeant	1400	No	
6. Staff Sergeant	2200	Yes	
7. Sergeant First Class	3000	No	
8. Master Sergeant	4000	Yes	
9. First Sergeant	5000	No	
10. Sergeant Major	6200	Yes	
11. Command Sergeant Major	7400	No	
12. Sergeant Major of the Army	8700	Yes	
13. Warrant Officer	10000	No	

Rank name	Points	Unlock	
14. Chief Warrant Officer	11500	Yes	
15. Second Lieutenant	13300	No	
16. First Lieutenant	15200	Yes	
17. Captain	17400	Yes	
18. Major	19700	No	
19. Lieutenant Colonel	22000	Yes	
20. Colonel	24200	Yes	
21. Brigadier General	26500	No	
22. Major General	28800	Yes	
23. Lieutenant General	31200	Yes	
24. General	33600	Yes	
25. General of the Army	37000	No	

As you increase in rank, you gain the ability to unlock weapons and gadgets which give you greater abilities and firepower. Each kit has two weapons and a gadget which can be unlocked by spending promotion credits. In addition, there is also one weapon per kit which is included in the Gold Edition of the game or can be unlocked by reaching the highest rank in the game. Finally one weapon per kit can be unlocked through promotional codes as part of the Find All Five promotion.

UNLOCKS BY KITS

Kit	Assault	Specialist	Recon	Support	Demolition
Basic Kit	Assault rifle	Compact rifle	Sniper rifle	Machine gun	Shotgun
	Hand grenade	Hand grenade	Pistol	Power tool	Hand grenade
	Grenade launcher	Tracer gun	Motion sensor	Medkit	Rocket launcher
Unlocks	Auto injector	C4 explosives	Laser designator	Mortar strike	AT Mine
	M16A2	UMP	SVU	XM8LMG	SPAS-12
	XM8	PP-2000	M95	MG36	Neostead
Gold Edition	AN94	XM8C	VSS Vintores	MG3	SPAS-15
Find All Five	F2000	Uzi	QBU88	M60	USAS12

PRIMA Official Game Guide

BATTLEFIELD BAD COMPANY

★ AWARDS ★

Players can earn a number of different types of awards while playing in ranked matches. In addition to collecting these awards, players will also receive points toward promotion in rank. Let's take a look at the awards you can earn.

TROPHIES

Trophies are awarded based on skills used during a round. They can be earned multiple times within a round as well as over the course of your career.

Trophies	In a Round Criteria	Score	Kit	
Assault Rifle Efficiency Trophy	6 Kills with Assault Rifle	10	Assault	
Grenadier Efficiency Trophy	3 Kills with Grenade Playing Assault	10	Assault	
Grenade Launcher Efficiency Trophy	6 Kills with Grenade Launcher	10	Assault	
M16 Efficiency Trophy	6 Kills with M16A2	10	Assault	
Marksman Trophy	5 Kills with Sniper Rifle	10	Recon	
Firearm Efficiency Trophy	3 Kills with Handgun	10	Recon	
Laser Designating Efficiency Trophy	3 Kills from Laser Designating	10	Recon	
SVU Efficiency Trophy	5 Kills with SVU	10	Recon	
Rocket Launcher Efficiency Trophy	3 Kills with Rocket Launcher	10	Demolitions	
Shotgun Efficiency Trophy	5 Kills with Shotgun	10	Demolitions	
Frag Out Efficiency Trophy	3 Kills with Grenade Playing Demolitions	10	Demolitions	
Mine Placement Efficiency Trophy	3 Kills with AT Mine	10	Demolitions	
Light Machinegun Efficiency Trophy	6 Kills with Light Machinegun	10	support	
Medic Trophy	20 Heal Points from Medkit (2 heals)	10	support	
Combat Engineer Trophy	20 Vehicle Repair Points (2 repairs)	10	Support	
Mortar Strike Efficiency Trophy	3 Kills with Mortar Strike	10	support	
Compact Assault Rifle Efficiency Trophy	6 Kills with Compact Assault Rifle	10	Specialist	
Target Tagging Efficiency Trophy	2 Kill Assists From Dartgun Tagging	10	Specialist	
Demo Pack Efficiency Trophy	3 Kills with C4	10	Specialist	
UMP Trophy	6 Kills with UMP	10	Specialist	
Explosive Efficiency Trophy	10 Kills with Explosives (Grenade Launcher, Hand Grenade, C4, LD, Mortar Strike, Rocket Launcher)	10	All	
Melee Combat Trophy (Dogtag)	5 Melee Kills (kills with a knife)	10	All	
Combat Efficiency Trophy	6 Kill Streak (kills in a row without dying)	10	All	
Kill Assist Trophy	5 Kill Assists	10	All	
Saviour Trophy	3 Saviour Point	10	All	
Avenger Trophy	3 Avenger Point	10	All	
High Card Trophy	Get the Best IAR Score	10	All	
Wheels of Hazard Trophy	2 Road Kills	10	All	
Transport Vehicle Trophy	5 Kills with Transport Vehicle	10	All	
Tank Warfare Trophy	5 Kills with Tanks	10	All	
Naval Surface Warfare Trophy	5 Kills with Sea Vehicle	10	All	
Combat Aviator Trophy	5 Kills with Air Vehicle	10	All	

Trophies	In a Round Criteria	Score	Kit	
Clear Skies Trophy	5 Kills with Air Defense	10	All	
Emplacement Trophy	5 Kills with Stationary Weapon	10	All	
Winning Team Trophy	Awarded in EOR	40	All	
Big Guns Trophy	5 Kills with Artillery	10	All	
Objective Destroyer Trophy	Destroy 3 Objectives	10	All	
Objective Attack Trophy	Destroy the Last Objective	10	All	
Objective Defender Trophy	30 Defend Bonus Points	10	All	
Squad Member Trophy	Assist or Save 5 Squad Members	10	All	
Squad Medication Trophy	40 Squad Member Heal Points (4 heals)	10	All	
Best Squad Trophy	Awarded in EOR	10	All	

PATCHES

Patches come in three types—bronze, silver, and gold. They are awarded for a combination of actions during a single round of play as well as trophies or other actions earned over the course of a career. Patches can only be awarded once.

Bronze Patches	In a Round Criteria	Other Criteria	Score	
Bronze Assault Patch	2 Kills as Assault	Assault Rifle Efficiency Trophy	20	
		Grenadier Efficiency Trophy		
		Grenade Launcher Efficiency Trophy		
Bronze Recon Patch	2 Kills as Recon	Marksman Trophy	20	
		Firearm Efficiency Trophy		
		Laser Designating Efficiency Trophy		
Bronze Demolitions Patch	2 Kills as Demolitions	Rocket Launcher Efficiency Trophy	20	
		Shotgun Efficiency Trophy		
		Frag Out Efficiency Trophy		
Bronze Support Patch	2 Kills as Support	Light Machinegun Efficiency Trophy	20	
		Medic Trophy		
		Combat Engineer Trophy		
Bronze Specialist Patch	2 Kills as Specialist	Compact Assault Rifle Efficiency Trophy	20	
		Target Tagging Efficiency Trophy		
		Demo Pack Efficiency Trophy		
Bronze Savior Patch	2 Saviour Point	x3 Savior Trophy	20	
Bronze Avenger Patch	2 Avenger Point	x3 Avenger Trophy	20	
Bronze Transport Vehicle Patch	2 Road Kills	x3 Transport Vehicle Trophy	20	
Bronze Tank Warfare Patch	Kill 2 Tanks in Tank Combat	x3 Tank Warfare Trophy	20	
Bronze Naval Surface Warfare Patch	Destroy 2 Naval Vehicles	x3 Naval Warfare Trophy	20	
Bronze Combat Aviator Patch	Kill 2 Helicopters in a Helicopter	x3 Combat Aviator Trophy	20	

Continued on next page

PRIMA Official Game Guide
BATTLEFIELD BAD COMPANY

PATCHES (CONTINUED)

Bronze Patches	In a Round Criteria	Other Criteria	Score	
Bronze Emplacement Patch	Kill 3 Vehicles and 3 Soldiers with Stationary Guns	x3 Emplacement Trophy	20	
Bronze Artillery Patch	1 Kill with Artillery	x3 Big Guns Trophy	20	
Bronze Attack Patch	Destroy One Objective	Objective Destroyer Trophy / Objective Attack Trophy	20	
Bronze Defend Patch	3 Kills as Defender	x3 Objective Defender Trophy	20	
Bronze Squad Patch	2 Squad Points	Squad Member Trophy / Squad Medication Trophy	20	

Silver Patches	In a Round Criteria	Other Criteria	Score	
Silver Assault Patch	2 Kills as Assault	Bronze Assault Patch; Assault Rifle Efficiency Trophy; Grenadier Efficiency Trophy; Grenade Launcher Efficiency Trophy; Carbine Efficiency Trophy	50	
Silver Recon Patch	2 Kills as Recon	Bronze Recon Patch; Marksman Trophy; Firearm Efficiency Trophy; Laser Designating Efficiency Trophy	50	
Silver Demolitions Patch	2 Kills as Demolitions	Bronze Demolitions Patch; Rocket Launcher Efficiency Trophy; Shotgun Efficiency Trophy; Frag Out Efficiency Trophy; Mine placement Efficiency Trophy	50	
Silver Support Patch	2 Kills as Support	Bronze Support Patch; Light Machinegun Efficiency Trophy; Medic Trophy; Combat Engineer Trophy; Mortar Strike Efficiency Trophy	50	
Silver Specialist Patch	2 Kills as Specialist	Bronze Specialist Patch; Compact Assault Rifle Efficiency Trophy; Target Tagging Efficiency Trophy; Demo Pack Efficiency Trophy; PP-2000 Trophy	50	

Silver Patches	In a Round Criteria	Other Criteria	Score	
Silver Savior Patch	2 Saviour Point	Bronze Savior Patch	50	
		x5 Savior Trophy		
Silver Avenger Patch	2 Avenger Point	Bronze Avenger Patch	50	
		x5 Avenger Trophy		
Silver Transport Vehicle Patch	2 Road Kills	Bronze Transport Vehicle Patch	50	
		x5 Transport Vehicle Trophy		
Silver Tank Warfare Patch	Kill 2 Tanks in Tank Combat	Bronze Tank Warfare Patch	50	
		x5 Tank Warfare Trophy		
Silver Naval Surface Warfare Patch	Destroy 2 Naval Vehicles	Bronze Naval Surface Warfare Patch	50	
		x5 Naval Warfare Trophy		
Silver Combat Aviator Patch	Kill 2 Helicopters in a Helicopter	Bronze Combat Aviator Patch	50	
		x5 Combat Aviator Trophy		
Silver Emplacement Patch	Kill 3 Vehicles and 3 Soldiers with Stationary Guns	Bronze Emplacement Patch	50	
		x5 Emplacement Trophy		
Silver Artillery Patch	1 Kill with Artillery	Bronze Artillery Patch	50	
		x5 Big Guns Trophy		
Silver Attack Patch	Destroy One Objective	x3 Objective Destroyer Trophy	50	
		x3 Objective Attack Trophy		
Silver Defend Patch	3 Kills as Defender	x6 Objective Defender Trophy	50	

Gold Patches	In a Round Criteria	Other Criteria	Score	
Gold Assault Patch	2 Kills as Assault	Silver Assault Patch	200	
		Assault Rifle Efficiency Trophy		
		Grenadier Efficiency Trophy		
		Grenade Launcher Efficiency Trophy		
		Carbine Efficiency Trophy		
		Melee Combat Trophy (Dogtag)		
Gold Recon Patch	2 Kills as Recon	Silver Recon Patch	200	
		Marksman Trophy		
		Firearm Efficiency Trophy		
		Laser Designating Efficiency Trophy		
		SVU Efficiency Trophy		
		Combat Efficiency Trophy		
Gold Demolitions Patch	2 Kills as Demolitions	Silver Demolitions Patch	200	
		Rocket Launcher Efficiency Trophy		
		Shotgun Efficiency Trophy		
		Frag Out Efficiency Trophy		
		Mine placement Efficiency Trophy		
		Avenger Trophy		

Continued on next page

PRIMA Official Game Guide

Gold Patches	In a Round Criteria	Other Criteria	Score	
Gold Support Patch	2 Kills as Support	Silver Support Patch	200	
		Light Machinegun Efficiency Trophy		
		Medic Trophy		
		Combat Engineer Trophy		
		Mortar Strike Efficiency Trophy		
		Saviour Trophy		
Gold Specialist Patch	2 Kills as Specialist	Silver Specialist Patch	200	
		Compact Assault Rifle Efficiency Trophy		
		Target Tagging Efficiency Trophy		
		Demo Pack Efficiency Trophy		
		Electronic Warfare Trophy		
		Explosive Efficiency Trophy		
Gold Savior Patch	2 Avenger Point	Silver Savior Patch	200	
		x7 Savior Trophy		
Gold Avenger Patch	2 Road Kills	Silver Avenger Patch	200	
		x7 Avenger Trophy		
Gold Transport Vehicle Patch	2 Road Kills	Silver Transport Vehicle Patch	200	
		x7 Transport Vehicle Trophy		
Gold Tank Warfare Patch	Kill 2 Tanks in Tank Combat	Silver Tank Warfare Patch	200	
		x7 Tank Warfare Trophy		
Gold Naval Surface Warfare Patch	Destroy 2 Naval Vehicles	Silver Naval Surface Warfare Patch	200	
		x7 Naval Warfare Trophy		
Gold Combat Aviator Patch	Kill 2 Helicopters in a Helicopter	Silver Combat Aviator Patch	200	
		x7 Combat Aviator Trophy		
Gold Emplacement Patch	Kill 3 Vehicles and 3 Soldiers with Stationary Guns	Silver Emplacement Patch	200	
		x7 Emplacement Trophy		
Gold Artillery Patch	1 Kill with Artillery	Silver Artillery Patch	200	
		x7 Big Guns Trophy		
Gold Attack Patch	Destroy One Objective	x6 Objective Destroyer Trophy	200	
		x6 Objective Attack Trophy		
Gold Defend Patch	3 Kills as Defender	x10 Objective Defender Trophy	200	
Gold Squad Patch	2 Squad Points	x6 Squad Member Trophy	200	
		x6 Squad Medication Trophy		

WILD CARDS

Wild cards are earned based on skill and various actions and trophies. They can only be awarded once.

Wild Card Patches	In a Round Criteria	Global Criteria	
Headshot	20 Kill from Headshot		
Gunslinger		80 Kills with Handgun	
Fly-by	4 Roadkills with Any Air Vehicle		
Dead Eye		Get 100 Headshots with Any Sniper Rifle	
Snake Eyes	11 Kills as 2 Different Classes		
Deuces are Wild	Kill 2 of Each Class		
Beat The House	15 Grenade Kills		
Armor Buster	Kill 5 Armor Vehicles	25 Total Armor Kills	
Tank Buster	Kill 5 Tanks	25 Total Tank Kills	
Chopper Chopper	Kill 5 Air Vehicles	25 Total Helicopter Kills	
1 on 1 Land	Destroy a Tank of the Same Kind without Any Assistance		
1 on 1 Sea	Destroy a Sea Vehicle of the Same Kind without Any Assistance		
1 on 1 Air	Destroy an Air Vehicle of the Same Kind without Any Assistance		
Straight Flush	Destroy 1 Vehicle of Each Kind		
Three of a Kind	Destroy 3 Vehicles of the Same Kind		
Five of a Kind	Destroy 5 Vehicles of the Same Kind		

Wild Card Patches	In a Round Criteria	Global Criteria	
Full House	Destroy 3 + 2 Vehicles of the Same Kind		
Cab Driver	5 Minutes as Driver in Vehicle with Passengers		
Airtime	2 Seconds Airtime with Land Vehicle		
Staying Dry	2 Seconds Airtime with Sea Vehicle		
Two Pair	Get 2 of Any 2 Trophies		
Santas Little Helper	10 Kill Assist Points and Total Kill Assist/Kill Ratio 2/1		
Full deck	52 Total Kills		
Saviour		50 Saviour Trophies	
Avenger		50 Avenger Trophies	
Destruction Site	Destroy 50 Objects		
Strike	Kill 10 Enemies at the Same Time		
Squad Wild Card	1 Squad Member Trophy per Squad Member and 10 Kills per Squad Member		
Squad Wild Card	Get 10 Squad Member Bonus Points	Become the Best Squad Once on Each Map	
Squad Avenger Card		Get 100 Avenger Kills Revenging Squad Members	

DOG TAGS

When you make a melee kill by eliminating an enemy using your knife, you collect their dog tags. In addition, you also receive a number of bonus points equal to their rank, ranging from 1 to 25 points. The dog tags for a kill will show the rank and name of the player you defeated.

PRIMA Official Game Guide

BAD COMPANY BATTLEFIELD

XBOX 360 ACHIEVEMENTS

Achievement	Description
Always get paid in gold bars	Complete "Welcome to Bad Company" on normal
Action, not words!	Complete "Welcome to Bad Company" on hard
Not even a nugget!	Complete "Acta Non Verba" on normal
Where are they going so fast?	Complete "Acta Non Verba" on hard
You and what army?	Complete "Crossing Over" on normal
Say goodbye to the gold!	Complete "Crossing Over" on hard
He might come in handy	Complete "Par for the Course" on normal
Cart wheels	Complete "Par for the Course" on hard
Hold on!	Complete "Air Force One" on normal
Russia?	Complete "Air Force One" on hard
Let's take the boat	Complete "Crash and Grab" on normal
Capitalist pigs, very nice	Complete "Crash and Grab" on hard
Sir, yes sir!	Complete "Ghost Town" on normal
Here is your DD-214	Complete "Ghost Town" on hard
You found it, you keep it	Find 5 unique collectables
Half-way thru	Find half of all collectables
Staying alive	Complete one mission without dying (any difficulty)
Killer on the loose	Kill 25 enemies
Death from above	Kill 25 enemies in a helicopter
Home wrecker	Destroy 200 walls
The hypochondriac	Use auto injector 50 times
Manic lumberjack	Knock down a small forest
The anti-mechanic	Destroy 50 vehicles (containing enemy AI)
Been there, drove that!	Drive all vehicle types (jeep, tank, helicopter, boat)
One in a million	Hit hostile helicopter with laser designator
Clean sweep	Find all collectables
I love gold!	Find one gold bar
Check my grill	Find half of the golden bars
Gold digger	Find all gold bars
On top of the world	Climb to the highest spot in the game
Get me started	(Online) Participate in one online match (Ranked)
Leatherneck	(Online) Play 100 online matches
Never used a door	(Online) Destroy 1000 walls
Forest ranger	(Online) Knock down 1000 trees
With my devil dogs	(Online) Use squad in the menu, find a friend, and play one round
There is no I in squad	(Online) Have 20 squad members spawn on you without dying in a single round
Dog owner!	(Online) Collect 5 unique dog tags
Get the dog!	(Online) Collect 50 unique dog tags
Be the best	(Online) Place #1 in a ranked match
Vehikill	(Online) Get at least one kill in every vehicle
Specialist	(Online) Reach Rank 3
Master Sergeant	(Online) Reach Rank 8
Colonel	(Online) Reach Rank 20
General of the Army	(Online) Reach Rank 25
Drive by	(Online) Get 100 kills using a vehicle
Catch the "Bad" moment	(Online) Take 3 pictures using the image system
Darwin's parachute	(Online) Glide in the parachute for 3 seconds
I am Bad Company!	(Online) Achieve all the awards
Ooh rah	(Online) Achieve half of all awards
Beans, bullets, bandages	(Online) Get 10002 kills